Happy Cooki*

& 

Enjoy the Food

Jof P.F

# Holiday & Entertainment

## COOKBOOK

# Holiday & Entertainment

## COOKBOOK

### RUDI SODAMIN

This publication contains the opinions and ideas of its author. It is intended to provide helpful and informative material on the subjects addressed in the publication. It is sold with the understanding that the author and publisher are not engaged in rendering medical, health, psychological, or any other kind of personal professional services in the book. If the reader requires personal medical, health, or other assistance or advice, a competent professional should be consulted.

The author and publisher specifically disclaim all responsibility for any liability, loss, or risk, personal or otherwise, that is incurred as a consequence, directly or indirectly, of the use and application of any of the contents of this book.

First published in the United States of America in 2002 by
Rizzoli International Publications
300 Park Avenue South
New York, NY 10010

2002 2003 2004 2005 2006/ 10 9 8 7 6 5 4 3 2 1

Printed in China

ISBN: 0-8478-2479-9

Library of Congress Catalog Control Number: 2002107068

This book is dedicated to all of the countless beautiful families
that have shared their holiday celebrations with the Royal Caribbean family
on board our magnificent ships, and to my own family.

# acknowledgments

Thank you to my wonderful wife and partner, Bente Sodamin, who tasted every dish and read every word, and who encouraged me to write this book. And to my children Magnus, Kenneth, and Kristina.

I also want to thank the following people: Pat Doyle who, along with Herb Schmitz, is an accomplished photographer and designer. Richard Fain, Daniel Hanarahn, Tom Murrill, Michael Bayley, Barbara Shrut, Lynn Martenstein, Corinne Lewis, Randi Galex, Dee Gretzler, Isidro Marfe, and Shedric Wallace. All Royal Caribbean Executive Chefs, Maître d's, F&B Managers, and Hotel Directors. I'd also like to thank my friend and colleague Marcelle Langan DiFalco, the best writer and editor, who helped me craft my thoughts and drafts into fine words. To Monica Velgos, my recipe editor extraordinaire, who made sure that the punctuation and style of each recipe is as concise as the measurements, *mille graci*. For their encouragement, I'd like to thank Sirio Maccioni and family, Michael and Ariane Batterberry, Zane Tankel, Patrick Beach, Steve Kirkpatrick, Jean Claude Peiffer, and Pepe Sanchez.

Thank you to my publisher at Rizzoli Charles Miers, along with Sheilah Ledwidge, Tricia Levi, and Lynne Yeamans.

# table of contents

# foreword

You will love this book! I admit it, I love it! It's hard not to get excited thinking about the holidays and picturing yourself throwing fabulous parties for your friends and loved ones.

Holidays are, by their very nature, special. They are celebrations of our lives—of who we are, of where we come from, and of the blessings we can count. Besides, anything that gives us a break from the run-of-the-mill, day-to-day grind is cause in and of itself to celebrate. As far as I'm concerned, there are not nearly enough holidays during the calendar year!

The special events of our lives do much more than bring us together with family and friends to enjoy food, get dressed up, and enjoy the present moment. They connect us with our past—with both our individual memories of family, as well as the larger rituals, traditions, and stories that bind us together as a nation, and even as human beings.

In fact, the holidays that I celebrated growing up in Austria in my family of twelve had a profound influence on my life. I vividly remember my mother cooking huge holiday feasts. I could see the great joy my mother took in nurturing, nourishing, and celebrating her large family—and we took incredible pleasure in our traditions and all her efforts.

When I'm traveling around the globe, people often ask me how they should celebrate a certain holiday, or what they should serve at a special party. My first suggestion, of course, is that they run (not walk) to book a cruise on Royal Caribbean International. I think that celebrating a holiday on a cruise ship is an experience no one should miss. I really think there is no better place to meet and celebrate a special occasion than on a Royal Caribbean ship. Just think of it: fabulous food, a beautiful ambiance, no cooking, no cleaning, a staff of hundreds to serve you, and nothing but time to enjoy yourself!

I have celebrated every holiday and family event under the sun with Royal Caribbean guests. It has made my culinary life richly textured with stories, faces, and places and has shaped my view of many cultures, traditions, and cuisines. I would not trade these experiences for anything. I've tried to capture as much of this as possible in the *Royal Caribbean Holiday & Entertainment Cookbook*, but there are many more holidays than I could possibly include in one volume. Nevertheless, I have presented a range of holidays and created simple, fool-proof menus for each along with historical insights and tips that will make entertaining at home as fabulous as it is aboard a Royal Caribbean ship.

Whether it's a banquet for a thousand on board a ship or an intimate dinner for two *chez moi*, I've learned that the difference between a good party and a great one lies in the details. Of course, a delicious menu made with the best ingredients is very important, but equally significant is the entire atmosphere you create for your guests.

First determine the style of the event. Is it formal? Casual? Will you serve dinner buffet style? Family style? Indoors? Outdoors? Then comes the fun part: figuring out ways to build on the style to make the party memorable and fun for your guests *and* yourself! Each chapter in this book has many tips for entertaining to get you started.

Once the decisions are made, the key to pulling all of your elements together beautifully—and keeping the frequent party-crasher called stress at bay—is planning, planning, planning!

The key to success for any party, no matter how big or small, is to keep lists and schedules: write the entire menu, including all finger foods and "extras" like lime wedges for the water pitcher; make a shopping list of everything you'll need; think of the special touches you'd like to include on your table, and in your living room, such as beautiful candles, and add any items that you might need to purchase to your shopping list. Then, create a realistic timeline/action plan that details when you will shop, prepare any menu items in advance, clean, choose serving pieces, and set the table. Be sure to include enough time to get dressed for the party and have a little quiet time before your guests arrive.

A well-laid, step-by-step plan will not only help you throw your best parties ever but will allow you to enjoy them even more. I hope this book gives you pleasure for a long time to come and enables you to make the most of your existing traditions and even create some new ones. I also hope it helps you achieve the kind of lasting holiday memories you will cherish forever.

Great books are always a collaborative effort. I want to thank the many people who have helped me bring this exciting book into your hands, especially Jack Williams, Adam Goldstein, and Maria Sastre, for their vision and support; Josef Jungwirth, who has cooked up a storm with me on the seven seas for many years; Dee Gretzler and Shedric Wallace, for supporting me with the Royal Culinary Collections; Corinne Lewis, for her tireless effort and support; and Herb Schmitz, the best food photographer on earth.

Wishing you smooth sailing!

Enjoy!
Rudi Sodamin
    Consulting Master Chef
    of Royal Caribbean International

# introduction

At Royal Caribbean International, entertaining is our business. Nobody on the seven seas does it better. For over thirty years, we have brought an unparalleled level of culinary quality, service, and attention to detail to our guests 365 days a year. They deserve the absolute best.

We feel especially honored when families entrust the celebration of their holidays to us aboard our magnificent ships. Whether it's a birthday, a family reunion, a major holiday, or Mother's Day, our international staff of hospitality experts makes the occasion deliciously memorable in every way possible.

Now, for the first time, we are delighted to share some of the holiday menus and memory-making secrets devised by guru of entertaining, Rudi Sodamin, our high-spirited culinary consultant and spokesperson, and Master Chef of Royal Caribbean International. Since joining Royal Caribbean several years ago, Rudi has been instrumental in bringing the culinary product up to a new level of excitement; he is truly a master in his field. Here, he has created a beautiful, easy-to-follow cookbook with creative menus and fresh tips for entertaining that bring the same exciting holiday dining experiences you can have on a Royal Caribbean cruise into your home.

We hope that you will be as inspired and enchanted by the *Royal Caribbean Holiday & Entertainment Cookbook* as we are to serve you whenever you board one of our beautiful ships.

From our family to yours, Happy Holidays!

Jack L. Williams

President and Chief Operating Officer, Royal Caribbean International and Celebrity Cruises

## TIP 1

Go for glamour when setting your table. Pick a color theme: black and white is classic but blue and silver can be just as dynamic.

## TIP 2

Line the center of the table with a series of unscented clear votives or a mix of multiple-sized pillar candles in a single color.

## TIP 3

Put small crystal bowls of fortune cookies on the dining room table for a fun diversion.

## TIP 4

Fill any extra champagne flutes or other elegant stemware with foil-wrapped chocolates and put one at each place setting.

## TIP 5

Turn on the CD player, with your pre-selected music programmed in. As soon as midnight arrives, play "Auld Lang Syne." Then switch to upbeat music.

## TIP 6

Send guests home with a surprise parting gift: a bag of a half-dozen fresh bagels and a quart of orange juice.

## TIP 7

Invest in some large mirrored tiles to use as place mats or indulge in purchasing chargers that match your color scheme.

## TIP 8

Have everyone write anonymous predictions for the new year and place them in a bowl. After midnight, read them aloud.

# New Year's Eve

When it comes to holidays, New Year's Eve is the granddaddy of them all. It was first celebrated in ancient Babylon about four thousand years ago, when the new year officially began with the first new moon after the vernal equinox (on the first day of spring). The Babylonians even made resolutions: the most common was to return borrowed farm implements.

In 46 B.C., Julius Caesar instituted the Julian Calendar. It established January 1, in early winter, as the official start to each new year. The rest, as they say, is history.

There are so many great ways to salute the old year and bring in the new that it's really hard to go wrong. For me, though, there is nothing like being at home for this holiday. I like to enjoy a fabulous meal surrounded by my nearest and dearest.

The menu for this dinner party is an indulgent and satisfying midwinter feast. Start with the Luscious Lobster Bisque. Lobster is one of those ingredients people consider a luxurious treat. The bisque is rich with cream, yet it's made ethereal with the lobster's brininess and my delicate spicing. The Globe Salad Splendour is a crisp prelude to the main course and a sunny nod to the first dawn of the new year.

The centerpiece of this menu is Garlic & Rosemary Steak with Potato-Onion Hash-Browned Cakes, a hearty, sizzling, sophisticated, and memorable entrée that's easy to prepare. As for dessert, nothing but the giddy lightness of an exquisite Chocolate Soufflé Cococay can reflect the spirit in which I think we should all start the new year. The Raspberry Radiance is a delightful spin on the traditional champagne toast.

# globe salad splendour
## with raspberry dressing

YIELD: 6 SERVINGS

### Globe Salad

6 RIPE BUT FIRM YELLOW OR
RED TOMATOES

1 BUNCH FRISÉE LETTUCE
(USE THE YELLOW SPRIGS)

1 BUNCH BABY OAK
LEAF LETTUCE

1 BUNCH AKAJISO SPROUTS

1 BUNCH BULLS
BLOOD BEET TOPS

1 BUNCH MAGENTA SPINACH

1 BUNCH BABY TATSOI

1 BUNCH POPCORN SHOOTS

1 BUNCH MIZUNA LETTUCE

1 BUNCH ENOKI MUSHROOMS

1 BUNCH BABY RED
ROMAINE LETTUCE

1 BUNCH CHIVES

Wash and dry all the ingredients very gently. Cut the tops from the tomatoes and hollow them out carefully, without breaking the tomato skin. Place the remaining salad components into each tomato, as if arranging flowers in a vase. Take your time because it will require patience. Chill, loosely covered, in the refrigerator until ready to serve.

### Raspberry Dressing

1 10-OUNCE (275 G) BAG
FROZEN RASPBERRIES,
THAWED AND SLIGHTLY
DRAINED, OR 1 PINT
FRESH RASPBERRIES

6 TABLESPOONS EXTRA
VIRGIN OLIVE OIL

3 TABLESPOONS
RASPBERRY VINEGAR

SALT AND FRESHLY GROUND
BLACK PEPPER TO TASTE

Combine all the ingredients in a blender and purée until thoroughly combined. Transfer to a container and refrigerate until ready to use.

### To assemble

To serve, place each globe salad on a plate and encircle with some of the raspberry dressing. Serve the remainder separately.

Note: Some of the salad ingredients are microgreens, available only from gourmet produce shops. Please don't let that stop you from making this beautiful salad. Feel free to substitute any other colorful ingredients that are more readily available.

Royal Culinary Collections®

This fine selection from Royal Culinary Collections
was especially developed for you by
Master Chef Rudi Sodamin

Raspberry
Balsamic
Vinegar
Gianni Calogiuri

Royal Caribbean
INTERNATIONAL

NET CONTENT 8.5 fl oz (250 ml)

# garlic and rosemary steak
## with potato-onion hash-browned cakes

### Marinated Steak

1/2 cup (125 ml) pure olive oil

1/2 cup (125 ml) soy sauce

1/4 cup (60 ml) balsamic vinegar
or red wine vinegar

8 large cloves garlic, minced

4 teaspoons dried rosemary, crumbled

1 2-inch-thick (5-cm) boneless top sirloin
steak, about 3 1/2 pounds (1.5 kg)

Salt and freshly ground black pepper to taste

Combine the oil, soy sauce, vinegar, garlic, and rosemary in a large glass baking dish. Add the steak and turn to coat. Season with salt and pepper. Cover and refrigerate overnight, turning a few times.

### Potato-Onion Hash-Browned Cakes

4 large baking potatoes, peeled

2 tablespoons minced onion

Salt and freshly ground black pepper to taste

4 tablespoons canola oil

1. Grate the potatoes right before cooking, so they won't discolor. In a bowl, combine the potatoes and the onions. Season with salt and pepper.

2. In a small nonstick skillet, heat a couple teaspoons oil over medium-high heat. Add about a cup of the potato mixture and flatten it evenly into a disk. Cook the potato cake until golden brown on each side.

3. Transfer to a plate lined with paper towels and keep warm until ready to serve. Repeat with the remaining oil and potato mixture.

### To Assemble

1/3 cup (75 ml) pure olive oil

2 large onions, cut into 1-inch pieces

2 red bell peppers, cored, seeded, and cut
into 1-inch (3-cm) pieces

3/4 teaspoon dried marjoram, crumbled

1/8 teaspoon crushed red pepper

Salt and freshly ground black pepper to taste

1. Remove the steak from the refrigerator and bring to room temperature. Meanwhile, heat the oil in a large heavy skillet over medium-high heat. Add the onions and sauté for 4 minutes. Add the peppers and sauté until they begin to soften, about 8 minutes. Add the marjoram and crushed red pepper. Season to taste with salt and pepper and cook, stirring, for 2 minutes. Remove from the heat.

2. Preheat the broiler for 5 minutes. Remove the steak from the marinade and pat dry. Transfer the marinade to a small heavy saucepan.

3. Broil the steak to the desired degree of doneness, about 10 minutes per side for rare. An instant-read thermometer inserted in the center should register 125°F (52°C) for medium-rare or 135°F (57°C) for medium. Transfer to a warmed platter, tent loosely with aluminum foil and let stand for 10 minutes.

4. To serve, reheat the bell peppers and onions in the skillet. Bring the marinade to a boil. Thinly slice the steak across the grain and arrange the slices on a platter. Surround with the peppers and onions and serve immediately, passing the marinade separately.

# luscious lobster bisque

3 TABLESPOONS PURE OLIVE OIL

1 POUND (450 G) LOBSTER
SHELLS, CUT INTO CHUNKS

1 MEDIUM SHALLOT, FINELY
MINCED

1 1/4 (300 ML) CUPS BRANDY

4 CUPS (1000 ML)
DRY WHITE WINE

1 CUP (140 G) FINELY DICED
ONION

3/4 CUP FINELY DICED CELERY

3/4 CUP FINELY DICED CARROT

2 MEDIUM CLOVES GARLIC,
FINELY CHOPPED

6 SPRIGS PARSLEY

2 SPRIGS TARRAGON

2 BAY LEAVES

2 1/2 CUPS CANNED CRUSHED
TOMATOES

3 QUARTS (3 L) FISH STOCK

SALT AND FRESHLY GROUND
WHITE PEPPER TO TASTE

2/3 CUP (150 G) UNSALTED
BUTTER, SOFTENED

1 1/4 CUPS (140 G)
ALL-PURPOSE FLOUR

1 1/4 CUPS (300 ML)
HEAVY CREAM

1/4 POUND (125 G) COOKED
LOBSTER MEAT, CHOPPED
(ABOUT 3/4 CUP)

1 SMALL BUNCH CHIVES,
CHOPPED

1. In a large wide saucepan, heat the oil over medium-high heat. Add the lobster shells and cook, stirring, until they turn red. Reduce the heat to medium and add the shallot. Cook, stirring, until the shallot softens and becomes translucent. (Do not let the shallot brown.)

2. Remove the saucepan from the stove and add the brandy. While standing at arm's length, place the saucepan over medium heat and carefully tilt it slightly away from the body to ignite the alcohol. (If you do not have a gas stove, carefully ignite the mixture with a match held at the edge of the saucepan, tilting it slightly away from the body.) Move the saucepan back and forth constantly until the flames die out. Simmer for 2 minutes.

3. Add the white wine. Remove the lobster shells and reserve. Add the onion, celery, carrot, garlic, parsley, tarragon, and bay leaves. Bring to a simmer and cook, stirring, for 3 minutes. Add the reserved lobster shells, tomatoes, and fish stock. Bring the mixture to a boil. Reduce the heat and simmer, stirring occasionally, for 30 minutes. Season with salt and pepper.

4. In a large bowl, mash the butter with the flour. Ladle some of the simmering liquid into the flour mixture and blend with a whisk. Pour the mixture back into the saucepan and continue to simmer, stirring, for 15 minutes. Remove the soup from the heat and strain it through a fine sieve into a clean saucepan.

5. Return the soup to the stove and bring to a simmer. Add the heavy cream and adjust the seasonings. To serve, divide the soup among warmed soup bowls. Garnish with the lobster meat and chopped chives.

# chocolate soufflé cococay

2 CUPS (500 ML) WHOLE MILK

1/2 CUP (115 G) GRANULATED SUGAR, PLUS EXTRA FOR DUSTING

4 TABLESPOONS UNSALTED BUTTER, PLUS EXTRA FOR GREASING

2 VANILLA BEANS, SPLIT

3/4 CUP (85 G) ALL-PURPOSE FLOUR

1/2 CUP (60 G) UNSWEETENED COCOA POWDER

3 OUNCES (90 G) SEMISWEET CHOCOLATE, CHOPPED

4 LARGE EGGS, SEPARATED

PREPARED CHOCOLATE SAUCE OR CRÈME ANGLAISE (SEE PAGE 162)

1. Preheat the oven to 400°F (200°C). Generously butter six 6-ounce (175 ml) soufflé dishes or ramekins. Dust the dishes with a little sugar; tilt to coat and tap out the excess. Set aside.

2. In a medium heavy saucepan, combine the milk, 1/4 cup of the sugar, and the butter over medium heat. Bring to a boil. Reduce the heat to low and use the tip of a blunt knife to scrape the vanilla bean seeds into the mixture. Gently simmer, stirring occasionally, until the vanilla has infused the mixture, about 15 minutes.

3. Add the flour and cook, stirring constantly, until the mixture leaves the sides of the saucepan clean, about 2 minutes. Remove from the heat and immediately add the cocoa powder and chopped chocolate. Whisk the mixture until it is smooth and no small lumps of chocolate remain. Let cool and transfer the mixture to a large bowl.

4. One by one, add the egg yolks to the milk mixture, beating well after each addition. (The mixture may be made ahead to this point, covered and refrigerated for up to 1 day. Bring to room temperature before proceeding.)

5. In a large, grease-free mixing bowl, beat the egg whites with an electric mixer on medium speed until frothy. Increase the speed to high and gradually add the remaining 1/4 cup sugar, beating until the egg whites form soft peaks.

6. Spoon one-third of the egg whites into the chocolate mixture and gently mix until the batter is lightened somewhat. With a rubber spatula, fold in the remaining egg whites, taking care not to deflate them.

7. Bring a large kettle of water to a boil. Line a roasting pan with a folded kitchen towel. Place the prepared soufflé dishes in the roasting pan and fill them three-fourths full with the soufflé mixture. Pour enough boiling water into the roasting pan to come one-third up the sides of the dishes. Bake for 20 minutes, or until doubled in height. Remove the dishes from the water bath and serve immediately with crème anglaise or chocolate sauce.

# raspberry radiance

YIELD: 8 SERVINGS

ICE CUBES, OPTIONAL

12 TABLESPOONS FRAMBOISE
LIQUEUR

2 TABLESPOONS PLUS
2 TEASPOONS FRESH
LEMON JUICE

1½ BOTTLES (1,125 ML TOTAL)
CHILLED BRUT CHAMPAGNE

1 PINT FRESH RASPBERRIES

Fill 8 champagne flutes with ice cubes. Pour 1½ tablespoons framboise liqueur and 1 teaspoon lemon juice into each flute. Fill the flutes with champagne. Garnish with raspberries and serve.

## FUN FACT!

Ringing in the New Year on a *Radiance of the Seas* cruise to the sunny Caribbean is a memorable experience. Many New Year's events are offered aboard this recent addition to Royal Caribbean International's fleet—from themed parties in every lounge to a countdown by the captain and a champagne toast. The environs are spectacular. Sweeping ocean vistas can be viewed through the floor-to-ceiling windows throughout the ship and glass elevators facing the sea.

## TIP 1

Supplement your Super Bowl buffet with platters of sliced pepperoni, cheeses, roasted red peppers, and marinated olives.

## TIP 2

Use heavy-duty coated paper plates for the hearty food being served.

## TIP 3

Decorate the buffet with pilsners or beer mugs filled with "tall" foods such as celery stalks, bread sticks, and pretzel rods.

## TIP 4

Beer is the beverage of choice for Super Bowl Sunday but also have soft drinks for designated drivers and other non-drinkers on hand. Place drinks in an ice-filled cooler.

## TIP 5

Use cushions from outdoor and other furniture for extra seating if you don't have enough space for all guests on your couches and chairs.

## TIP 6

Keep food out and available from the kickoff, but put the main dishes on the buffet during the half-time break.

## TIP 7

Make sure your thermostat is not set too high. While it may feel a bit chilly at first, it will soon become comfortable once everyone is there.

## TIP 8

Collect Super Bowl trivia questions and see if you can stump the fans during the half-time show.

# Super Bowl Party

The Super Bowl provides a perfect excuse to throw a party. Even if you don't watch another football game all year, it's a great opportunity to gather friends for food and fun.

For many Americans Super Bowl Sunday is like a high holy day. And that's no surprise. After all, it's not just a game—it's a cultural phenomenon. The first Super Bowl, between the Green Bay Packers and the Kansas City Chiefs, took place on January 15, 1967. (Green Bay trounced Kansas City 35 to 10.) This culmination of each year's professional football season has been a national institution ever since.

Like all great American holidays, food traditions have evolved around the event. The first rule of play is that there must be lots of finger food. The second rule is that spicy, saucy, finger-licking dishes are served. As with all my menus, this lineup has something for everyone. Start with the addictive Spiced Peanuts, which can be made in advance. The Apricot & Garlic Barbecued Chicken Drumettes are another delicious appetizer and a nice change from Buffalo wings.

The buffet table also includes delicious dips and a homey Chicken Chili (a perfect midwinter dish for any occasion). Keep the Super Bowl Punch on the buffet as a crisp refreshment to serve with these intensely bold foods. No matter which team prevails, Touchdown Brownies are certain to be a winner with all of your biggest fans.

# spiced peanuts

2 TEASPOONS VEGETABLE OIL

1 1/2 TEASPOONS CAJUN SEASONING
OR CHILI POWDER

1/4 TEASPOON CAYENNE PEPPER

2 CUPS LIGHTLY SALTED DRY-ROASTED PEANUTS

**1.** Heat the oil in a large heavy skillet over medium heat. Stir in the Cajun seasoning and cayenne and cook for a few seconds.

**2.** Add the peanuts and cook for 2 minutes, stirring constantly. Transfer to a plate lined with a paper towel to drain briefly. Serve warm or at room temperature. (Can be stored, tightly covered, for up to 3 weeks.)

# apricot & garlic barbecued chicken drumettes

YIELD: 4 SERVINGS

1 CUP (250 ML) APRICOT
NECTAR

1/4 CUP (60 ML) TOMATO PASTE

1/4 CUP (60 ML) HONEY

1/2 SERRANO PEPPER, STEMMED,
SEEDED, AND MINCED

2 TABLESPOONS APPLE
CIDER VINEGAR

2 TABLESPOONS
WORCESTERSHIRE SAUCE

2 TEASPOONS FINELY CHOPPED
GARLIC

1/2 TEASPOON SALT

2 POUNDS (900 G) CHICKEN
DRUMETTES (ABOUT 16),
SKIN REMOVED

1 TEASPOON CHOPPED PARSELY

**1.** Heat the oven to 375°F (190°C). In a small bowl, combine all the ingredients except the parsley and chicken. Mix well.

**2.** Arrange the drumettes in a single layer in a 9 x 13-inch (23 x 32-cm) baking pan. Pour the sauce over the chicken and bake for 20 to 25 minutes, basting occasionally, until the chicken is no longer pink and is glazed nicely. Sprinkle with chopped parsely, and serve immediately.

# dill dip delight

1 CUP (250 ML) SOUR CREAM

1 CUP (250 ML) PREPARED OR HOMEMADE
MAYONNAISE (SEE RECIPE PAGE 28)

3 CLOVES GARLIC, FINELY CHOPPED

6 TABLESPOONS CHOPPED FRESH DILL

6 TABLESPOONS CHOPPED FRESH PARSLEY

SALT AND FRESHLY GROUND PEPPER TO TASTE

Combine all the ingredients except for the salt
in a nonreactive bowl. Whisk to blend. Season
with salt and freshly ground pepper. Cover
and refrigerate for at least 1 hour to allow the
flavors to develop.

# vision veggie dip

YIELD: 3 CUPS

1 TABLESPOON UNSALTED BUTTER

1 10-OUNCE (283-G) PACKAGE FROZEN CHOPPED
SPINACH, THAWED AND SQUEEZED DRY

2 CUPS (500 ML) SOUR CREAM

3/4 CUP (170 ML) PREPARED OR HOMEMADE
MAYONNAISE (SEE RECIPE PAGE 28)

2 TEASPOONS DIJON MUSTARD

1 TEASPOON VEGETABLE SPICE BLEND (ROYAL
CULINARY COLLECTIONS) OR A DASH OF CELERY
SALT, WHITE PEPPER, AND DRIED ONIONS

1 8-OUNCE (227-G) CAN SLICED WATER CHESTNUTS,
DRAINED AND CHOPPED

3 GREEN SCALLIONS, FINELY CHOPPED

SALT AND FRESHLY GROUND BLACK PEPPER
TO TASTE

1 ROUND COUNTRY-STYLE BREAD LOAF,
TOP SLICED OFF AND LOAF HOLLOWED OUT

1. In a medium skillet, heat the butter over
medium heat. Add the spinach and cook,
stirring, until lightly sautéed, about 2 minutes.
Transfer to a large bowl and let cool.

2. Add the sour cream, mayonnaise, mustard,
and spice blend to the spinach. Stir until well
combined. Stir in the water chestnuts and
scallions. Season with salt and pepper. Cover
and refrigerate for at least 2 hours to allow
the flavors to develop.

3. To serve, stir the dip once more and then
spoon it into the hollowed out bread. Arrange
bread cubes, crackers, or fresh cut vegetables
around the bread bowl for dipping.

# empress herb extravaganza

YIELD: 2 CUPS

1 CUP (250 ML) PREPARED OR HOMEMADE
  MAYONNAISE (SEE RECIPE BELOW)

1 CUP (250 ML) SOUR CREAM

1/2 CUP (125 ML) TOMATO PURÉE

2 TABLESPOONS FRESH LEMON JUICE

1/4 CUP CHOPPED FRESH PARSLEY

1/4 CUP CHOPPED FRESH DILL

2 CLOVE GARLIC, MINCED

2 TABLESPOONS MINCED SCALLIONS

2 TEASPOONS MINCED FRESH CHIVES

1 TEASPOON DRIED TARRAGON LEAVES

WORCESTERSHIRE SAUCE TO TASTE

SALT AND FRESHLY GROUND BLACK PEPPER
  TO TASTE

In a nonreactive bowl, combine all the ingredients except for the Worcestershire sauce, salt, and pepper. Whisk to blend. Season with the remaining ingredients. Cover and refrigerate for at least 1 hour to allow the flavors to develop. Serve with chips or vegetables.

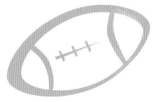

# homemade mayonnaise

YIELD: 2 CUPS

Refrigerate this mayonnaise as soon as it's made and be sure to store it no longer than 3 to 4 days.

4 LARGE EGG YOLKS

1 TEASPOON SALT

1 TEASPOON GRANULATED
  SUGAR

1/4 TEASPOON WHITE PEPPER

1/4 TEASPOON PAPRIKA

2 TABLESPOONS FRESH LEMON
  JUICE

2 TABLESPOONS WHITE VINEGAR

2 CUPS (500 ML) VEGETABLE
  OIL

1. In a food processor, combine the egg yolks, salt, sugar, pepper, and paprika. Blend until thick. Add the lemon juice and vinegar, and blend until combined.

2. With the motor running, add the oil very slowly through the feed tube, stopping once or twice to scrape down the sides. The mixture should become very thick. Adjust the seasonings. Transfer to a container. Cover and refrigerate until ready to use.

Note: The following dip recipes are enjoyable simply with chips—even vegetables chips—or with a wide range of raw or crisp-cooked vegetables. Suggestions include: artichoke hearts, asparagus spears, Belgian endive leaves, carrot sticks, cauliflower or broccoli florets, celery sticks, cucumber or zucchini sticks, daikon radish sticks, scallions, snow peas, and sugar snap peas. Just make sure that what you choose is fresh and at peak flavor.

# super bowl punch

YIELD: 2 QUARTS

1 BOTTLE DRY RED WINE

1/2 CUP (125 ML) RUM

1 LEMON, WASHED AND SLICED
  INTO ROUNDS

1 ORANGE, WASHED AND SLICED
  INTO ROUNDS

1 LIME, WASHED AND SLICED
  INTO ROUNDS

1 PINT STRAWBERRIES, RINSED
  AND THICKLY SLICED

1 APPLE, CORED AND CUT INTO
  1/2-INCH (1-CM) SLICES

7 WHOLE CLOVES

1 LITER LEMON/LIME-FLAVORED
  SODA

1. In a large nonreactive pitcher, combine the wine, rum, citrus slices, and strawberry slices. Push the cloves into the apple slices and add to the mixture. Cover and refrigerate for at least 4 hours or overnight.

2. To serve, strain the wine mixture into some tall glasses, filling them halfway. Fill the rest of each glass with the flavored soda and stir gently. Remove the cloves from the apple slices and garnish the drinks by spooning some of the marinated fruit into the glasses.

# chicken chili cozumel

YIELD: 4 SERVINGS

1 TABLESPOON EXTRA VIRGIN OLIVE OIL

1¹/2 POUNDS (650 G) BONELESS, SKINLESS CHICKEN
BREAST, ROUGHLY CHOPPED OR GROUND

1 CUP CHOPPED YELLOW ONION

1¹/2 CUPS (375 ML) CHICKEN BROTH

1 4-OUNCE (113-G) CAN GREEN CHILE PEPPERS,
CHOPPED

1 TEASPOON GARLIC POWDER

1 TEASPOON GROUND CUMIN

¹/2 TEASPOON DRIED OREGANO

¹/2 TEASPOON GROUND CORIANDER

¹/8 TEASPOON CRUSHED RED PEPPER

2 15-OUNCE (452-G) CANS WHITE NAVY BEANS,
DRAINED AND RINSED

SALT AND FRESHLY GROUND BLACK PEPPER
TO TASTE

3 SCALLIONS, CHOPPED

³/4 CUP GRATED MONTEREY JACK CHEESE

1 CUP TOMATOES, FINELY CHOPPED

2 JALAPEÑO PEPPERS, THINLY SLICED

**1.** Heat the oil in a large pot over medium-high heat. Add the chicken and yellow onion and sauté for 4 to 5 minutes.

**2.** Add the stock, chile peppers, garlic powder, cumin, oregano, coriander, and crushed red pepper. Bring to a boil. Reduce the heat to low and simmer, stirring occasionally, for 15 minutes.

**3.** Stir in the beans and simmer for 10 minutes more. Season with salt and pepper. To serve, divide among 4 bowls and top with the scallions, cheese, chopped tomato, and jalapeño slices.

**Note:** Make this dish a day ahead and reheat.

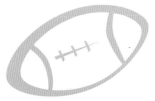

## FUN FACT!

Many cruises to the western Caribbean take you to the port of Cozumel, an island off the coast of Mexico. Activities here include touring the ancient Mayan ruins of Tulúm (the only Mayan site next to the ocean) and arguably the most famous Mayan site of all, Chichén Itzá. Cozumel also has unparalleled snorkeling opportunities, which include viewing the natural limestone formations of the Xal-ha Lagoon.

# touchdown brownies

5 OUNCES (140 G) UNSWEETENED CHOCOLATE, CHOPPED (ABOUT 1 CUP)

1/2 CUP (115 G) UNSALTED BUTTER, PLUS EXTRA FOR GREASING

1/2 CUP (115 G) VEGETABLE SHORTENING

3 EXTRA-LARGE EGGS

3 CUPS (675 G) GRANULATED SUGAR

1 CUP (110 G) ALL-PURPOSE FLOUR

13 OUNCES (375 G) CARAMELS, UNWRAPPED (ABOUT 45)

1/3 CUP (75 ML) EVAPORATED MILK

12 OUNCES (340 G) SEMISWEET CHOCOLATE CHIPS

1/3 CUP CHOPPED WALNUTS OR PECANS

CONFECTIONERS' SUGAR FOR DUSTING

1. Preheat the oven to 350°F (180°C). Lightly coat a 9 x 13-inch (23 x 33-cm) baking pan with butter.

2. Place the chocolate, butter, and shortening in the top of a double boiler set over 1 inch (3 cm) of simmering (not boiling) water. Whisk until the chocolate is smooth and no small lumps remain. Remove the mixture from the hot water (keep the water simmering). Let cool.

3. In a mixing bowl, combine the eggs and sugar. With an electric mixer, beat until pale in color, about 5 to 10 minutes, stopping 2 or 3 times to scrape down the sides of the bowl. With a rubber spatula, fold in the chocolate mixture. Sift the flour over the batter and fold it in just until incorporated (do not overmix).

4. Pour three-fourths of the batter into the prepared baking dish and bake for 6 minutes. Meanwhile, melt the caramels with the evaporated milk in the top of the double boiler set over the simmering water.

5. Sprinkle partially baked brownies with the chocolate chips and nuts. Pour the melted caramel mixture over the top and spoon the remaining brownie batter over the surface.

6. Bake the brownies for 30 minutes more. Let cool in the pan on a wire rack. Cut into 16 squares, place on a serving platter, and dust them with confectioners' sugar.

## FUN FACT!

Innovative self-leveling pool tables found on *Radiance of the Seas* can be enjoyed while watching the Super Bowl half-time show—or at any other time. In addition, the ship includes many other opportunities to enjoy sports (when not watching the big game) including rock climbing two hundred feet above the sea, miniature golf, basketball, swimming, and more.

**TIP**
# 1
Keep all the overhead lights in the house turned off to create a romantic mood. If you have dimmers, use them to turn the lights low.

**TIP**
# 2
Set up a cozy table for two in an area of the house where you don't usually eat, such as by a fireplace.

**TIP**
# 3
As a special treat, purchase an after-dinner drink: Port, Cognac, Sauternes, Prosecco—or a sweet wine or digestif.

**TIP**
# 4
Choose a selection of your favorite romantic music— a mix of instrumentals and jazz vocals is perfect. Keep the music playing continuously.

**TIP**
# 5
Fill a bucket with ice and chill a nice bottle of premium champagne (half bottles or "splits" are now available on premium labels).

**TIP**
# 6
Use special china or tableware. Oversized plates and linen napkins are luxurious and replicate the feel of a fine restaurant.

**TIP**
# 7
Make a centerpiece by nestling a thick bunch of red and white flowers into a crystal bowl. Surround the bowl with votives.

**TIP**
# 8
On a beautiful silver tray, bring out an assortment of petit fours and/or premium chocolates. A final decadent treat.

# Valentine's Day

Seduction, spice, and romance are the three words that come to mind when I think of this holiday. It's one of the busiest days of the year in luxury restaurants and there's a good reason why: Great food flames passion.

Valentine's Day is devoted to lovers. I think it's so important to celebrate Valentine's Day in style because frequently it is our most significant relationship that takes a back burner to everything else in our daily lives. Valentine's Day should be the one holiday that commands our most undivided attention when it comes to the details.

The legend of Valentine's Day demonstrates just how seriously we should take love. The holiday dates back to Ancient Rome when the date of February 14 was designated to honor the queen of Roman goddesses, Juno. Each boy would draw the name of a girl who would then be his partner for the festivities. Sometimes these matches would end up in marriage. These rituals were later banned by the Emperor Claudius who prohibited marriage. He believed men would not go to war because they would not want to leave their lovers or families. The legend has it that Saint Valentine, a Roman priest, married couples in secret. This was a crime for which he was executed on the fourteenth day of February. Today, he is the patron saint of lovers.

My idea of a perfect Valentine's evening is an intimate dinner at home. For this menu, I've used some of the foods that I think of as being particularly seductive and appropriate for the occasion: a steamy, creamy seafood risotto and a sensuous and satisfying Tenderloin for Two that has extra heat and spice from a Peppercorn Sauce. Since a traditional Valentine's Day gift is chocolate, I've included a decadent treat: Chocolate Dipped Fruit. This can be served with store-bought chocolate truffles and petits fours. You can add to the intimacy of the evening by cooking the meal together.

# savory sweetheart's salad

YIELD: 8 SERVINGS

1 POUND (450 G) MIXED BABY LETTUCES
OR MESCLUN GREENS

4 CHERRY TOMATOES, QUARTERED

1/2 MEDIUM SHALLOT, FINELY CHOPPED

3 TABLESPOONS RED WINE VINEGAR

1 TABLESPOON DIJON MUSTARD

1 TEASPOON GRANULATED SUGAR

1/3 CUP (75 ML) EXTRA VIRGIN OLIVE OIL

SALT AND FRESHLY GROUND BLACK PEPPER TO TASTE

Gently wash and dry the greens and place in a large salad bowl with the tomatoes. In a nonreactive bowl, combine the shallot, vinegar, mustard, and sugar. Slowly whisk in the oil until emulsified. Season with salt and pepper. When ready to serve, toss the salad greens with just enough dressing to coat.

# risotto frutti de mare

YIELD: 4 TO 6 SERVINGS

1 QUART (1 L) FISH STOCK

1/4 POUND (125 G) BABY SHRIMP, UNPEELED

1/4 POUND (125 G) BAY SCALLOPS

1 TABLESPOON UNSALTED BUTTER

1/4 CUP DICED ONION

1 CUP ARBORIO RICE

1/2 CUP (125 ML) DRY WHITE WINE

3/4 CUP GRATED PARMESAN CHEESE

SALT AND FRESHLY GROUND WHITE PEPPER TO TASTE

CHOPPED FRESH PARSLEY FOR GARNISH

1. In a medium saucepan, bring the fish stock to a boil. Add the shrimp and cook, stirring, for 30 seconds. With a slotted spoon, transfer to a small bowl. Repeat the procedure for the scallops. Reduce the heat and hold the stock at a low simmer. Peel and devein the shrimp and set the seafood aside.

2. In a medium cast iron skillet, heat half the butter over medium-low heat. Add the onion and cook, stirring, until the onion is softened, about 2 minutes. Add the rice and stir with a wooden spoon until a toasted aroma develops, about 4 minutes.

3. Add one-third of the simmering stock and cook, stirring constantly, until the liquid evaporates. Add half the remaining stock and cook, stirring constantly, until the liquid evaporates. Repeat this procedure for the remaining stock and the wine, cooking and stirring after adding each, until the liquid evaporates. The risotto should be creamy but still slightly firm in the center.

4. Add the reserved shrimp and scallops, the remaining butter and Parmesan. Cook, stirring, until the seafood is heated through. Season with salt and pepper. Serve the risotto in warmed bowls. Garnish with chopped parsley.

# tauranga tenderloin for two
## with peppercorn sauce

YIELD: 2 SERVINGS

1 TABLESPOON EXTRA VIRGIN
  OLIVE OIL

1 14-OUNCE (400 G) BEEF
  TENDERLOIN

SALT TO TASTE

2 TABLESPOONS TOMATO PASTE

1/4 CUP (60 ML) BRANDY

1 LARGE CLOVE GARLIC, MINCED

1 TEASPOON MULTICOLORED
  PEPPERCORNS, CRUSHED

PINCH DRIED OREGANO

1/8 TEASPOON SALT

2/3 CUP (150 ML) WHIPPING
  CREAM

1 TABLESPOON SOUR CREAM

HOT COOKED RICE

2 SPRIGS FRESH OREGANO
  FOR GARNISH

FRESHLY CRACKED PEPPER
  TO TASTE

**1.** Heat the oil in a medium skillet until hot. Sprinkle the steaks with salt and pepper.

**2.** Place the tenderloin in the hot skillet and sear until well browned, about 2 minutes per side. Transfer from the skillet to the rack of a broiler pan. Reserve skillet drippings. Broil 5 1/2 inches (15 cm) from the heat (if using an electric oven, keep the door partially open) for 5 to 7 minutes per side, or until an instant-read thermometer registers 140°F/60°C for rare, 150°F/66°C for medium-rare, or 160°F/71°C for medium.

**3.** Meanwhile, add the tomato paste to the drippings in the skillet and cook for 1 minute until golden brown. Add the brandy and bring to a boil. Scrape up any browned bits from the bottom of the skillet and stir to dissolve them. Add the minced garlic, peppercorns, oregano, and salt to taste. Cook for 1 minute.

**4.** Add the whipping cream and bring to a boil over medium heat. Reduce the heat and simmer, stirring occasionally, until the sauce is reduced by half, about 6 to 7 minutes.

**5.** Remove from the heat and whisk in the sour cream. To serve, spoon the sauce over the steaks and serve with hot rice. Garnish with oregano sprigs and sprinkle with freshly cracked pepper.

## FUN FACT!

What's a Tauranga? It's just one of the ports of call on Royal Caribbean International's cruises to New Zealand. From here, guests can visit Rotorua, a city rich in Maori heritage, as well as the unusual boiling mud pools of Whakarewarewa Thermal Reserve. Additional ports are Christchurch, Dunedin, and Hobart. The ship also travels through Fjordland National Park, where guests can enjoy the fertile landscape and spectacular waterfalls from aboard the ship. While on the cruise, couples can renew their wedding vows. More than 2,000 couples a year take their wedding vows on Royal Caribbean ships.

VALENTINE'S DAY

# chocolate dipped fruit

YIELD: 8 SERVINGS

2½ POUNDS (1.2 KG) SEMISWEET CHOCOLATE, CHOPPED INTO ¼-INCH (.5-CM) CHUNKS

1 POUND (450 G) RED SEEDLESS GRAPES, STEMMED, WASHED, AND DRIED

¾ POUND (350 G) DRIED PINEAPPLE SLICES

¾ POUND (350 G) DRIED PEACH HALVES

¾ POUND (350 G) DRIED PEAR HALVES

2 PINTS STRAWBERRIES WITH STEMS, LIGHTLY RINSED AND DRIED

1. Line 2 baking sheets with parchment paper; set aside. Place 1 pound (450 g) chocolate in the top of a double boiler and tightly cover with plastic wrap. Set over 1 inch (3 cm) of water and heat over medium heat for 12 minutes.

2. Remove the chocolate from the heat and let stand for 5 minutes before removing plastic wrap. With a rubber spatula or whisk, stir until smooth. Continue to stir until the temperature of the chocolate is reduced to 90°F (32°C).

3. Place the grapes in a stainless steel bowl and pour the melted chocolate over them. With a fork, transfer the chocolate-drenched grapes, one by one, onto the prepared baking sheets. Refrigerate for 10 to 15 minutes, until the chocolate has hardened. Transfer the grapes to the center of a large serving platter and refrigerate.

4. Repeat steps 1 and 2 with another pound (450 g) of chocolate. One at a time, dip ½ inch to 1 inch (1 to 3 cm) of each dried fruit into the melted chocolate. Allow excess chocolate to drip back into the double boiler before placing the fruit onto the prepared baking sheets. Refrigerate for 10 to 15 minutes, until the chocolate has hardened. Arrange the chocolate-dipped fruit near the outside edge of the large serving platter and return it to the refrigerator.

5. Repeat steps 1 and 2 with the remaining ½ pound (225 g) chocolate and the strawberries. Holding by the stem end, dip ½ inch to 1 inch (1 to 3 cm) of each berry, one at a time, into the melted chocolate. Allow excess chocolate to drip back into the double boiler before placing the fruit onto the prepared baking sheets. Refrigerate for 10 to 15 minutes, until the chocolate has hardened.

6. Arrange the chocolate-dipped strawberries between the grapes and the dried fruit on the serving platter and return it to the refrigerator. Keep chilled until 10 minutes before serving.

## TIP
### 1

Adapt this menu to create a brunch buffet, if you prefer. Add a favorite quiche and fresh scones and rolls.

## TIP
### 2

Plan your color scheme to match the burgeoning season: the pale pastels of new leaves, tulips, daffodils, crocuses, and lilacs.

## TIP
### 3

Dye hard-boiled eggs to match your color scheme and place them in a pedestaled pie plate with Easter grass. This makes a lovely centerpiece.

## TIP
### 4

Fold your napkins into large triangles and place one on each plate. Fill individual egg cups with tiny gourmet jelly beans and put one atop each napkin.

## TIP
### 5

Place ivory taper candles in candlesticks of different heights. Put these in between the centerpiece and flowers (crocuses, tulips, and roses are beautiful).

## TIP
### 6

Play music in the background. Gregorian chants are wonderful for the occasion, as is Vivaldi's *Four Seasons*.

## TIP
### 7

Easter egg art isn't just for children—hand-designed eggs make pretty, whimsical decorations for the table.

## TIP
### 8

Fill plastic Easter eggs with a premium chocolate or two. When it's time to serve dessert, offer the adults these special sweet treats.

# Easter Sunday

For thousands of years, Easter has been a time of great joy and celebration. Not only is the day the most important in the Christian liturgical year, but it signals the launch of the season of renewal and rebirth.

Easter has been a holy Christian celebration of the resurrection of Christ since the second century A.D. For hundreds of years prior to this, it was a pagan ritual commemorating the goddess of fertility and springtime, Eastre, who was symbolized by the rabbit. The concept of the Easter egg also predates the Christian holiday. From the earliest days of recorded history, the egg has been a symbol of rebirth in most cultures. Peasants boiled eggs with brightly colored leaves or flower petals, and gave them as presents during these early spring festivals.

Easter is really the last major holiday until Thanksgiving that inspires me to host a formal affair. In the later spring and summer, holiday entertaining tends to be casual. Positioned as it is in early spring, my Easter menus are always a mix of heartier fare, like tasty stews and glazed meats, alongside lighter dishes. The menu here is one of my favorites for this time of year. It starts with a delicious spinach tart inspired by the classic Greek Easter food, spanakopita (spinach, onions, and feta cheese in phyllo dough). Lamb is another time-honored traditional Easter food, and here I've put it into a delicate white stew. The sinfully sweet chocolate mousse rounds out this meal.

# enchantment ensalada

YIELD: 8 SERVINGS

2 HEADS BIBB OR BOSTON LETTUCE

2 SCALLIONS, THINLY SLICED

1 RIPE TOMATO, CORED, SEEDED, AND CUT INTO JULIENNE STRIPS

2 LARGE HARD-COOKED EGGS, PEELED AND QUARTERED

1. Gently wash and dry the lettuce leaves. Place them in a bowl with the scallions and tomato. Sprinkle enough lemon dressing over the salad to lightly coat the leaves.

2. To serve, divide the salad among 8 chilled salad plates. Place an egg quarter on each plate and sprinkle it with some dressing. Serve immediately.

### Lemon Dressing

1/3 CUP (75 ML) FRESH LEMON JUICE

2 TABLESPOONS MINCED SHALLOTS

1 TEASPOON GRANULATED SUGAR

1 TEASPOON SALT

1/2 TEASPOON FRESHLY GROUND BLACK PEPPER

1/2 TEASPOON MILD MUSTARD

1 CUP (250 ML) EXTRA VIRGIN OLIVE OIL

In a nonreactive bowl, whisk the lemon juice, shallots, sugar, salt, pepper, and mustard. Slowly whisk in the oil. (Alternatively, combine all the ingredients in a screw-top jar and vigorously shake until thoroughly mixed.) Cover and refrigerate until ready to use.

## FUN FACT!

To make your own Easter egg dye, combine food coloring with 1 teaspoon of white vinegar and 1/2 cup (125 ml) boiling water. For a stripe effect, twist a combination of thin and wide rubber bands lengthwise and crosswise around a hard-cooked egg to make a free-form design. Dip the egg into dye, let dry completely, then remove the bands.

# tortola spinach tart
## with spicy tomato coulis

### Tart Shell

1½ CUPS (170 G) ALL-PURPOSE FLOUR

¼ TEASPOON SALT

8 TABLESPOONS VEGETABLE SHORTENING, CHILLED

3 TO 4 TABLESPOONS ICE WATER

1 LARGE EGG WHITE, BEATEN WITH 1 TABLESPOON WATER

**1.** In a large bowl, combine the flour and salt. Using your fingertips, a pastry blender, or 2 knives, work the shortening into the flour until the mixture resembles coarse meal. (Alternatively, combine the ingredients in a food processor, using short pulses.)

**2.** With a fork, stir in just enough of the water to gather the mixture into a soft ball of dough. Pat into a disk, cover with plastic wrap, and chill in the refrigerator for at least 1 hour or up to 3 days.

**3.** On a lightly floured surface, roll out the dough into a round ⅛-inch (3-mm) thick. Drape the dough over a rolling pin and fit it into a 9-inch (23-cm) pie pan. Fold the edge under and crimp. Place the pie shell in the freezer for 20 minutes, while preheating oven to 360°F/185°C. Remove the shell and prick it all over with the tines of a fork to prevent bubbling during baking.

**4.** Place a piece of aluminum foil over the dough and fill it with pie weights or dried beans. Place the shell in the oven and bake for 6 minutes. Remove the foil and brush the sides and bottom of the shell with the egg white wash. Return to the oven and bake for an additional 8 to 10 minutes. Place on a wire rack and let cool before filling.

## Spicy Tomato Coulis

1½ POUNDS (700 G) RIPE TOMATOES

⅔ CUP (150 ML) EXTRA VIRGIN OLIVE OIL

10 MEDIUM CLOVES GARLIC, CRUSHED

⅓ CUP FINELY CHOPPED SHALLOT

1 BOUQUET GARNI (1 BAY LEAF, 2 SPRIGS OF
THYME, 2 SPRIGS OF PARSLEY, BUNDLED IN A
PIECE OF CHEESECLOTH AND TIED WITH STRING)

PINCH OF GRANULATED SUGAR

6 BLACK PEPPERCORNS, CRUSHED

SALT TO TASTE

1. In a medium saucepan, bring 2 quarts (2 L) water to a boil. With a paring knife, cut out the stems from the tomatoes and make a small X in the opposite ends. Plunge the tomatoes in the boiling water and leave them in just until the skins are loosened, 10 to 20 seconds. With a slotted spoon, transfer the tomatoes to a bowl of cold water to cool. Slip off the skins and cut the tomatoes in half. Gently but firmly squeeze the seeds from the halves. Chop the tomatoes.

2. In a large skillet, heat the oil over medium heat. Add the garlic, shallot, and bouquet garni. Cook, stirring, until the shallot softens and becomes translucent, about 2 minutes. Add the chopped tomatoes, sugar, and peppercorns and bring to a simmer. Reduce the heat to very low and simmer, stirring occasionally with a wooden spoon, until all the liquid is evaporated, about 1 hour.

3. Remove and discard the bouquet garni. Transfer the tomato mixture to a blender and purée until smooth. Strain through a fine sieve into a saucepan and keep warm at the back of the stove.

## To Assemble

1 TABLESPOON UNSALTED BUTTER

1 MEDIUM ONION, CHOPPED

1 10-OUNCE (275 G) PACKAGE FROZEN SPINACH,
THAWED

3 LARGE EGGS, LIGHTLY BEATEN

½ CUP (125 ML) HEAVY CREAM

1 CUP (250 ML) WHOLE MILK

SALT AND FRESHLY GROUND WHITE PEPPER
TO TASTE

1. Preheat the oven to 350°F (180°C). In a large sauté pan, heat the butter over medium heat. Add the onion and cook, stirring, until softened and translucent. Add the spinach and sauté until most of the liquid is evaporated. Remove from the heat.

2. In a medium bowl, whisk the eggs, cream, and milk. Season with salt and pepper. Spread the spinach mixture in the bottom of the prepared pie shell and pour the egg mixture over it.

3. Bake the tart for 25 to 30 minutes, or until lightly browned and set. Remove from the oven and let cool for a few minutes. To serve, cut into wedges and serve on top of a puddle of spicy tomato coulis.

# legend-ary lamb
## with white beans, sage, and wild mushrooms

YIELD: 6 SERVINGS

1 POUND (450 G) DRIED
GREAT NORTHERN BEANS,
PICKED OVER FOR STONES

6 1-POUND (450 G) LAMB
SHANKS, CRACKED BY THE
BUTCHER

SALT AND FRESHLY GROUND
BLACK PEPPER TO TASTE

3 TO 4 TABLESPOONS
ALL-PURPOSE FLOUR

3 TO 4 TABLESPOONS
EXTRA-VIRGIN OLIVE OIL

2 CUPS CHOPPED ONION

1/2 CUP CHOPPED CARROT

6 LARGE CLOVES GARLIC,
MINCED

1/3 CUP COARSELY CHOPPED
FRESH SAGE

1 1/2 CUPS (375 ML)
DRY RED WINE

1 1/4 CUPS (310 ML)
CHICKEN STOCK

2 TABLESPOONS UNSALTED
BUTTER

1/4 CUP FINELY CHOPPED
SHALLOT

6 OUNCES (170 G) FRESH
CHANTERELLE MUSHROOMS,
TRIMMED, WIPED CLEAN,
AND CUT INTO THIN STRIPS

6 OUNCES (170 G) FRESH
SHIITAKE MUSHROOMS,
STEMMED, WIPED CLEAN,
AND CUT INTO THIN STRIPS

1/4 POUND (112 G) FRESH
BLACK TRUMPET MUSHROOMS,
WIPED CLEAN

ROSEMARY SPRIGS FOR GARNISH

1. Place the beans in a large saucepan and add enough water to cover them by 2 inches (5 cm). Bring to a boil over medium-high heat. Reduce the heat to low and simmer the beans for 2 minutes. Turn off the heat, cover the saucepan, and let stand at room temperature for 1 hour. Drain the beans, discarding the soaking liquid.

2. Preheat the oven to 350°F (180°C). Pat the lamb shanks dry with paper towels. Season with salt and pepper and dredge in the flour, shaking off the excess.

3. In a large heavy skillet, heat the oil over medium-high heat. Add the shanks, in batches, and sauté until browned on all sides. (Add more oil to later batches if necessary.) With a pair of tongs, transfer the shanks as each is browned to a large flameproof casserole or Dutch oven.

4. Add the onion, carrot, and garlic to the skillet and cook, stirring, over medium heat until the onion softens and becomes translucent, about 5 to 7 minutes. Add the sage and sauté for 1 minute. Add the drained beans, wine, and chicken stock and scrape up any browned bits from the bottom of the pan. Transfer the contents of the skillet to the casserole.

5. Bake the shanks, covered, for 1 1/2 to 2 hours, or until the meat is tender. Just before the shanks are done, heat the butter in a large skillet over medium-high heat. Add the shallot and sauté for 2 minutes. Add the mushrooms and cook, stirring, until the mushrooms are soft and the liquid in the pan is almost evaporated, about 5 minutes.

6. With a pair of tongs, transfer the lamb shanks to a warmed serving platter and tent with aluminum foil to keep warm. Skim the fat from the surface of the beans. Stir in the mushroom mixture and adjust the seasonings. Pour the beans and mushrooms over the shanks and serve immediately, garnished with a sprig of rosemary.

# melbourne velvet mousse

1 TEASPOON UNFLAVORED
GELATIN

1 TABLESPOON COLD WATER

2 TABLESPOONS BOILING WATER

$1/2$ CUP (115 G) GRANULATED
SUGAR

$1/4$ CUP (30 G) UNSWEETENED
COCOA POWDER

1 CUP (250 ML) WHIPPING
CREAM

1 TEASPOON PURE VANILLA
EXTRACT

CHOCOLATE SHAVINGS
FOR GARNISH

1. In a small bowl, sprinkle the gelatin over the cold water and let stand for 1 minute. Add the boiling water and stir until the gelatin is dissolved.

2. In a mixing bowl, combine the sugar, cocoa powder, whipping cream, and vanilla. With an electric mixer, beat on medium speed until the mixture is stiff, stopping 2 or 3 times to scrape down the sides of the bowl.

3. Add the gelatin mixture and beat until well blended. Spoon into dessert dishes or champagne glasses. Sprinkle with shaved chocolate. Chill, covered, for at least 1 hour before serving.

## FUN FACT!

Melbourne is just one of the cities to visit on the exotic destinations tours aboard *Legend of the Seas*, which travels to Australia, New Zealand, French Polynesia, and Hawaii. In the 1850s, Melbourne was settled by British gold seekers. Today it's a cosmopolitan and culturally mixed city with excellent shopping and restaurants. Spending a day touring Melbourne is easy and fun—trams are definitely the way to travel here.

**TIP**

**1**

Use formal linen tablecloths and napkins for this festive occasion.

**TIP**

**2**

Put out small shallow bowls filled with salt water for dipping. *Karpas* and *Chazeret* are dipped in the water, which represents tears.

**TIP**

**3**

Be sure to have enough wine and grape juice on hand—four cups are consumed by each guest. Today, there are excellent kosher wines.

**TIP**

**4**

Line the center of the table with your prepared seder plate, a cup for Elijah, the cloth-covered three pieces of matzo, and the wine bottles or carafes.

**TIP**

**5**

Print out copies of the *Haggadah* on beautiful paper, secure with twine, and insert a sprig of parsley into the knot.

**TIP**

**6**

Roast the shank bone for the seder plate for 30 minutes.

**TIP**

**7**

If children will be at the seder, have them make decorations: place mats, napkin rings, or place cards.

**TIP**

**8**

At the end of the meal, have children try to find the matzo half that is broken by the narrator and hidden.

# Passover

This is the most widely observed of all the holidays on the Jewish calendar. For this celebration, food is indispensable to the telling of a story that's over three thousand years old.

There are many rituals associated with the observance of Passover. They are derived from the Book of Exodus in which Moses warned Egyptian Pharaoh Ramses II that if he didn't free the Israelites from slavery, God would unleash a series of ten plagues on Egypt. After the first nine plagues, the Pharaoh had not relented. The final plague was the slaying of the first-born male in each household. After the Israelites were spared, and the Pharaoh's own son was taken, Ramses II agreed to end the enslavement.

To commemorate this event, Jewish people celebrate Passover, or Pesach. The holiday begins with a lavish meal called a seder, which is filled with traditions and conducted in a very organized fashion. The requisite centerpiece of the festive holiday is the seder plate, which holds the six foods that are symbols of the struggle of the Israelites: *Charoset* (a mixture of apples, nuts, wine and spices); *Zeroa* (a shank bone); *Baytzah* (hard-boiled egg); *Karpas* (usually parsley); *Maror* (bitter herbs, usually horseradish); and *Chazeret* (a bitter vegetable, usually celery). Next to the seder plate, three pieces of matzo are placed in a matzo cover (a cloth sleeve or covered plate).

The *Haggadah* is read at the service. It contains the story of the exodus from Egypt; explanations of symbolic objects on the seder table; and the prayers, psalms, and songs of Passover.

The Passover menu here, with its Chopped Chicken Liver, Roast Turkey Breast with Vegetables and Rosemary Potatoes, and Vegetable Farfel Kugel, incorporates traditional Jewish cookery with a modern spicing.

# chopped chicken liver

YIELD: 6 SERVINGS

2 TABLESPOONS MARGARINE

3 SPANISH ONIONS, THINLY
  SLICED

1 POUND (450 G) CHICKEN
  LIVERS

2 LARGE HARD-COOKED EGGS,
  PEELED AND ROUGHLY
  CHOPPED

SALT AND FRESHLY GROUND
  BLACK PEPPER TO TASTE

6 SLICES TOAST, CUT IN HALF
  DIAGONALLY

1 TEASPOON FINELY CHOPPED
  PARSLEY

LETTUCE LEAVES, TOMATO
  WEDGES, AND RED ONION
  RINGS AS GARNISH

1. In a large heavy skillet, heat 1 tablespoon margarine over medium heat. Add the onions and cook, stirring, until lightly browned. Transfer to a bowl.

2. In the same skillet, heat the remaining 1 tablespoon margarine. Add the chicken livers and sauté until no longer pink inside. Add the livers to the onions and let cool.

3. In a food processor, combine the onions, livers, and eggs. Pulse until the mixture is chopped, taking care not to purée it. (Alternatively, chop the mixture in a meat grinder using the coarse blade.) Season with salt and pepper.

4. Divide the chopped liver, toast, and garnish ingredients among 6 plates. Serve immediately.

PASSOVER

54

# charoset

2 MEDIUM APPLES, 1 TART AND
1 SWEET

1/4 CUP (40 G) FINELY CHOPPED
ALMONDS AND WALNUTS

1 CUP RAISINS

1 TABLESPOON GROUND
CINNAMON

1/4 CUP (60 ML) DRY RED WINE

1/4 CUP (60 ML) SWEET
RED WINE

1. Peel the apples and grate them into a nonreactive bowl. Add the chopped almonds and walnuts, raisins, and cinnamon and mix well.

2. Slowly stir in the wine until the mixture forms a paste. Cover and let stand for 3 to 6 hours, until the wine is absorbed by the other ingredients. Serve with horseradish on matzo.

Note: This fruit, nut, and wine mixture is eaten during the Passover seder. It is meant to remind us of the mortar used by Jewish people to build the cities of Egypt during the period of their slavery.

# vegetable farfel kugel

YIELD: 12 SERVINGS

NONSTICK COOKING SPRAY

2 CUPS MATZO FARFEL

1 CUP (250 ML) WATER

2 TABLESPOONS UNSALTED
MARGARINE

1/2 CUP CHOPPED SPANISH
ONION

1/2 CUP CHOPPED CARROT

1/2 CUP CHOPPED CELERY

1 CUP CHOPPED WHITE
MUSHROOMS

1 CUP CHOPPED ZUCCHINI

2 TABLESPOONS CHOPPED
FRESH PARSLEY

1 TEASPOON SALT

FRESHLY GROUND BLACK PEPPER
TO TASTE

6 LARGE EGGS

1. Preheat the oven to 325°F (170°C). Coat a 9 x 13-inch
(23 x 32-cm) baking dish with nonstick spray.

2. Soak the matzo farfel in the water until soft. Squeeze out any
excess water and place the mixture in a large bowl. Set aside.

3. In a sauté pan, heat the oil. Add the onion, carrot, and celery.
Cook, stirring, until the onion becomes softened and translucent,
about 5 minutes.

4. Add the mushrooms and zucchini. Cook, stirring, for 5 more
minutes. Transfer the contents of the pan to the bowl with the
farfel. Add the parsley and salt. Toss to combine. Season to taste
with pepper. Let the mixture cool slightly and then stir in the eggs.

5. Transfer the mixture to the prepared baking dish and bake
for 1 hour. Remove from the oven and let it sit for 10 minutes
before cutting and serving.

# bergen beet salad
## with orange dressing

YIELD: 4 SERVINGS

### Orange Dressing

4 TABLESPOONS ORANGE
 JUICE, FRESH OR FROM
 CONCENTRATE

2 TABLESPOONS WHITE WINE
 VINEGAR

1/4 TEASPOON GRATED
 ORANGE ZEST

2 TABLESPOONS EXTRA VIRGIN
 OLIVE OIL

SALT AND FRESHLY GROUND
 WHITE PEPPER TO TASTE

In a nonreactive bowl,
combine the orange juice,
vinegar, and orange zest.
Slowly whisk in the oil.
Season with salt and pepper.
Cover and refrigerate until
ready to use.

### Beet Salad

4 BUNCHES BEETS, ROOT ENDS TRIMMED AND TOPS REMOVED

1 TABLESPOON SALT

1. Wash the beets, taking care not to pierce the skin. In a large
steamer, bring some water and the salt to a boil. Place the beets
in the steamer and cook, covered, until a knife easily enters
the beets, about 40 minutes. (Add water occasionally if it has
evaporated too much.)

2. Transfer the beets to a colander and run under cool water. Slip
off the skins (use gloves if you don't want to stain your hands).
Slice into fine strips or dice into cubes.

3. Toss the beets gently with the orange dressing. Cover and
refrigerate for several hours. Adjust the seasonings, if necessary,
before serving.

## FUN FACT!

On the British Isles/Norwegian Fjords cruises aboard
*Brilliance of the Seas*, Bergen, Norway, is one of the many
spectacular ports of call. Bergen is Norway's second-largest
city and is in a beautiful natural setting surrounded by
seven mountains. Visitors see medieval stone churches,
sparkling fjords, and rugged glacier scenery. In addition,
the cruise ship stops at many other locales throughout
Norway, including Geiranger, Flåm, and Oslo.

# roast turkey breast
## with vegetables and rosemary potatoes

YIELD: 6 SERVINGS

### Turkey

1 3$^1$/$_2$-POUND (1.6-KG) TURKEY
  BREAST WITH SKIN

4 TABLESPOONS PURE OLIVE OIL

1 TEASPOON FRESH THYME
  LEAVES, CHOPPED

1 TEASPOON SWEET PAPRIKA

KOSHER SALT AND FRESHLY
  GROUND BLACK PEPPER
  TO TASTE

4 SPRIGS FRESH ROSEMARY

2 POUNDS (900 G) SMALL RED
  POTATOES, WASHED WELL

2 TEASPOONS FRESH ROSEMARY
  LEAVES, CHOPPED

1 CUP (250 ML) CHICKEN STOCK

1 POUND (454 G) CHERRY
  TOMATOES

1. Preheat the oven to 400°F (200°C). Place the turkey breast in a flameproof roasting pan. In a small bowl, combine 1 teaspoon oil, the thyme, paprika, salt, and pepper. Rub the mixture on the turkey skin. Tuck some rosemary sprigs under the skin.

2. Cut the potatoes in half and place them in a medium bowl. Add the chopped rosemary and sprinkle with 1 teaspoon olive oil. Season with salt and pepper and toss to coat.

3. Roast the turkey breast, uncovered, for 15 minutes. Baste with chicken stock and add the potatoes to the pan. Reduce the heat to 360°F (185°C) and continue to roast the turkey, basting occasionally, for about 30 minutes more. Turn the potatoes.

4. About 15 minutes after turning the potatoes, add the cherry tomatoes and any stock, if necessary, to the roasting pan. Continue roasting until an instant-read thermometer inserted into the thickest part of the breast registers 170°F (75°C).

5. Transfer the turkey and tomatoes from the roasting pan to a warmed serving platter. Check the potatoes: if they are not yet tender, continue to roast until they are done and then add them to the platter. Tent the turkey and vegetables with aluminum foil to keep warm and let rest for 30 minutes. Reserve the juices.

### Gravy and Vegetables

1 CUP (250 ML) DRY
  WHITE WINE

1 CUP (250 ML) CHICKEN STOCK

2 TABLESPOONS POTATO
  STARCH

SALT AND FRESHLY GROUND
  BLACK PEPPER TO TASTE

24 SPEARS ASPARAGUS,
  FIBROUS ENDS REMOVED

1 TABLESPOON FRESH PARSLEY,
  CHOPPED

1. Pour the juices into a glass cup. Skim off and discard the fat. Set aside. Place the roasting pan over low heat and add the wine. Scrape up any browned bits from the bottom of the pan. Add the chicken stock and cook, stirring, for 2 to 3 minutes.

2. Whisk in the reserved turkey juices and potato starch. Cook, stirring constantly, until the gravy thickens and bubbles, about 2 minutes. Strain the gravy through a medium sieve into a saucepan and bring to a boil over high heat. Reduce the heat to low and simmer, stirring, until the gravy lightly coats the back of a spoon. Adjust the seasonings with salt and pepper, and keep warm.

3. Bring a large saucepan of salted water to a boil. Add the asparagus and cook until tender. To serve, stir the parsley into the gravy, and slice the turkey breast. Serve the potatoes and vegetables alongside.

# chocolate fudge nut torte

UNSWEETENED COCOA POWDER
  FOR DUSTING

1 12-OUNCE (340 G) BAG
  SEMISWEET CHOCOLATE CHIPS

1/2 CUP (115 G) UNSALTED OR
  PAREVE MARGARINE

5 LARGE EGGS, SEPARATED

1 TABLESPOON PURE VANILLA
  EXTRACT

1/4 CUP (55 G) GRANULATED
  SUGAR, PLUS EXTRA FOR
  GARNISH

1 PINT RASPBERRIES

1. Preheat the oven to 250°F (130°C). Lightly grease an 8-inch (20-cm) springform pan. Dust the pan with a little cocoa; tilt to coat and tap out the excess. Set aside.

2. Place the chocolate chips and margarine in the top of a double boiler set over 1 inch (3 cm) of simmering (not boiling) water. Whisk until the chocolate is smooth. Turn off the heat and remove the mixture from the hot water.

3. In a large bowl, whisk the egg yolks with the vanilla. Slowly whisk the warm melted chocolate into the yolks until well blended.

4. In a large, grease-free mixing bowl, beat the egg whites with an electric mixer on medium speed until frothy. Increase the speed to high and gradually add the sugar, beating until the egg whites form stiff peaks.

5. Spoon one-third of the egg whites into the chocolate mixture and gently mix until the batter is lightened somewhat. With a rubber spatula, fold in the remaining egg whites, taking care not to deflate them.

6. Pour the mixture into the prepared pan and bake for 1 hour, or until a skewer inserted in the center comes out clean. Transfer the pan to a wire rack and let cool in the pan.

7. To serve, unmold the cooled torte onto a plate and cut into 12 slices. Sprinkle with sugar and garnish with raspberries.

## TIP 1

Set the table with your mother's favorite cloth or a well-loved antique damask cloth or a pretty pastel cotton cloth.

## TIP 2

Roll place settings of silverware in pastel or white cloth napkins and secure with pieces of ribbon tied in bows with long tails.

## TIP 3

Keep hot coffee and tea available throughout the meal. Use cups with saucers, and set out real cream and light milk.

## TIP 4

Spring is one of the loveliest times of year. If possible, set the table outdoors to enjoy spring's natural beauty and abundance—and glorious ambiance.

## TIP 5

Type an attractive menu and personalize it for your mother: include the date, your mother's name, all the dishes, and the name of the chef(s).

## TIP 6

Line miniature bud vases down the center of the table and fill with flower buds that match or contrast with the color of your linens.

## TIP 7

Set the stage for lingering: place a basket with local newspapers and magazines in the area where you will be sitting.

## TIP 8

Mothers always notice the details. Fill a beautiful carafe with ice water and slices of lemon and lime.

# Mother's Day

Mother's Day, one of the loveliest holidays on the calendar, is a day to honor and thank mothers by catering to them from start to finish. There's no better way to celebrate than to start the day with a delicious brunch.

One of the things I love about preparing brunch is the relaxed, light-hearted spirit of the occasion. The time of day during which brunch is served, typically late morning through mid-afternoon, allows moms to enjoy a leisurely morning in bed while the cooking is done by others. A long, laid-back, multiple-course meal designed for lingering around the table ensues.

This menu combines both breakfast and lunch favorites: Eggs Benedict hails from the breakfast table. The poached salmon and polenta with sun-dried tomatoes straddle beautifully from breakfast to lunch fare. The Braised Yankee Pot Roast is pure comfort food, perfect for the leisurely meal. Finally, Linzer Torte, a favorite pastry from my native Austria, rounds out the menu.

Set up a buffet with the salmon, polenta, and pot roast. You can also add any number of other elements to the buffet table such as fresh bagels and muffins, as well as jams and cheeses. I cook the Eggs Benedict to order so they are piping hot. It only takes a few minutes to cook the eggs after you've prepared the ingredients in advance.

# eggs benedict

## Hollandaise Sauce

YIELD: ABOUT 1 CUP

1/2 POUND (225 G)
  UNSALTED BUTTER

2 TABLESPOONS FINELY
  CHOPPED SHALLOTS

3 TABLESPOONS WHITE
  WINE VINEGAR

8 BLACK PEPPERCORNS,
  CRUSHED

3 LARGE EGG YOLKS

1 TABLESPOON FRESH
  LEMON JUICE

SALT TO TASTE

HOT PEPPER SAUCE (SUCH
  AS TABASCO) OR CAYENNE
  PEPPER TO TASTE

1. Clarify the butter: Melt the butter in a medium saucepan over low heat. Cook until the butterfat becomes clear and the milk solids drop to the bottom of the pan. Skim the surface foam as the butter separates. Carefully spoon the clear butterfat into a second saucepan and keep warm. Discard the milky liquid at the bottom of the first saucepan.

2. In a small nonreactive saucepan, combine the shallots, vinegar, and peppercorns over medium heat. Cook, stirring, for 2 to 3 minutes. Strain and discard the solids.

3. Transfer the shallot liquid to the top of a double boiler set over 1 inch (2.5 cm) of simmering (not boiling) water. Add the egg yolks and gently cook, whisking constantly,

until the eggs become thick, frothy, and pale in color. (Do not let the sauce come to a boil.) Blend in the lemon juice and season with salt and hot pepper sauce or cayenne pepper.

4. Turn off the heat and remove the mixture from the hot water. Slowly drizzle in the warm clarified butter, whisking constantly, until the sauce thickens into the consistency of heavy cream. Strain through a fine sieve into a warmed bowl and adjust the seasonings. (Use a little warm water to thin the sauce if necessary.) Keep warm or serve immediately.

### To Assemble

2 ENGLISH MUFFINS, SPLIT IN HALF

UNSALTED BUTTER AS NEEDED

4 2-OUNCE (55 G) SLICES CANADIAN BACON OR COOKED HAM, HEATED

4 LARGE EGGS, POACHED (SEE NOTE AND SIDEBAR)

Toast the muffin halves and spread with butter. Divide them among 4 warmed plates. Top each muffin half with a slice of Canadian bacon or ham and a well-drained poached egg. Ladle the hollandaise sauce over the top and serve immediately.

Note: To get the best results with poached eggs, use the freshest eggs available. Fresh eggs maintain their shape best because the whites and yolks are firm. With poached eggs, the object is to keep the eggs in a round, compact mass rather than spread them out.

## POACHED EGG TIPS

If the eggs are not very fresh, add 1 teaspoon salt and 2 teaspoons distilled vinegar per quart of water. The vinegar helps coagulate the whites faster, so they keep a better shape.

Bring water to a simmer in a wide saucepan. If the water boils, the eggs will toughen and may be broken up by the agitation. If the water is not hot enough, the eggs will not cook quickly enough and will spread.

Break the eggs one at a time into a dish or a small plate and slide into the simmering water.

Simmer 3 to 5 minutes until the whites are coagulated and the yolks are still soft. Remove the eggs from the water with a slotted spoon.

To serve the eggs immediately, drain well. To hold them until later, plunge them immediately into a bowl of cold water and ice to stop the cooking. When ready to serve, reheat the eggs briefly in hot water.

# pisa polenta
## with sun-dried tomatoes, garlic, corn, and caramelized onions

YIELD: 4 SERVINGS

### Polenta

2 1/2 CUPS (625 ML) WATER

1 TEASPOON KOSHER SALT

2 TEASPOONS EXTRA VIRGIN OLIVE OIL

1 TEASPOON MINCED GARLIC

2 TEASPOONS MINCED FRESH SAGE

1/4 CUP FRESH CORN KERNELS

2 TABLESPOONS CHOPPED SUN-DRIED TOMATOES (NOT PACKED IN OIL), SOAKED IN WARMED WATER TO COVER FOR 10 TO 15 MINUTES

3/4 CUP YELLOW CORNMEAL

NONSTICK COOKING SPRAY

1. In a heavy saucepan, bring the water and salt to a boil over high heat. Meanwhile, in a small nonstick sauté pan, heat the oil over medium heat. Add the garlic and sage and cook, stirring, until the garlic softens, 2 to 3 minutes. Scrape the contents of the sauté pan into the boiling water. Add the corn kernels and sun-dried tomatoes and reduce the heat to medium, so that the liquid just simmers.

2. Handful by handful, add the cornmeal to the water in a steady rain, whisking constantly, until fully incorporated with no lumps. Cook, whisking constantly, until thick and bubbly, about 5 to 7 minutes. Remove from the heat.

3. Coat a 5 x 9-inch (12.5 x 23-cm) loaf pan with nonstick cooking spray. Pour the polenta into the pan, smooth the surface, and spray it lightly with the vegetable oil spray. Cover with plastic wrap and let cool.

### Caramelized Onions

1 TEASPOON EXTRA VIRGIN OLIVE OIL

3 LARGE RED ONIONS, THINLY SLICED

1 TABLESPOON PURE MAPLE SYRUP OR LIGHTLY PACKED LIGHT BROWN SUGAR

1 TABLESPOON BALSAMIC VINEGAR

2 TEASPOONS DRIED BASIL

2 TABLESPOONS VEGETABLE STOCK

1. In a nonstick sauté pan, heat the oil over high heat. Add the onions and cook, stirring constantly, until deep golden brown, caramelized and soft, about 10 minutes. Adjust the heat if needed so the onions don't burn.

2. Stir in the maple syrup or brown sugar, vinegar, basil, and vegetable stock and reduce the heat. Keep warm at the back of the stove until ready to use.

### Tomato Concassé

2 TEASPOONS EXTRA VIRGIN OLIVE OIL

2 TEASPOONS MINCED GARLIC

4 MEDIUM TOMATOES, CORED AND DICED

1 TEASPOON KOSHER SALT

1/4 TEASPOON FRESHLY GROUND BLACK PEPPER

1/4 CUP CHIFFONADE OF FRESH BASIL

In a sauté pan, heat the oil over high heat. Add the garlic and cook for a few seconds. Quickly stir in the tomatoes. Cook, stirring, just until the tomatoes are heated through. Add the salt, pepper, and basil. Cover and keep warm until ready to use.

## To Assemble

NONSTICK COOKING SPRAY

3/4 CUP FROZEN OR FRESH SHELLED PEAS

1/2 CUP FRESH CORN KERNELS

1/2 CUP DICED CELERY

1/2 CUP DICED CARROT

1/4 CUP SLICED SCALLIONS

2 TEASPOONS CRUMBLED FETA CHEESE (OPTIONAL)

CHOPPED FRESH PARSLEY FOR GARNISH

1. Preheat the oven to 300°F (150°C). Heat a charcoal or gas grill to medium. Lightly coat a baking sheet and the grill top with nonstick cooking spray. Invert the polenta onto a work surface and cut into 8 triangles or squares. Grill the polenta on both sides only until well marked, about 2 to 3 minutes on each side.

Transfer to the prepared baking sheet in a single layer and bake for 4 to 5 minutes in the oven, until heated through. Remove from the oven and sprinkle with the feta cheese, if desired.

2. Meanwhile, combine the peas, corn, celery, and carrot in the top of a steamer set over 1 inch (2.5 cm) of boiling water. Cover and steam until the vegetables are fork-tender, 3 to 5 minutes. Transfer to a warmed bowl and stir in the scallions.

3. To serve, ladle the tomato concassé in the center of each warmed plate. Place 2 squares of polenta on the concassé and top with the caramelized onions. Surround with the steamed mixed vegetables and sprinkle with chopped parsley. Serve immediately.

# skagway salmon
## with mustard sauce

YIELD: 4 SERVINGS

2/3 cup (150 ml) dry
  white wine

1 scallion, chopped (reserve
  green tops for garnish)

4 6-ounce (175 g) skinless
  salmon fillets, about
  1 inch (3 cm) thick

1 pound (450 g) fresh
  spinach leaves

1 tablespoon butter

1/2 cup (120 ml) heavy or
  whipping cream

1 tablespoon plus
  1 teaspoon Dijon mustard

Salt and freshly ground
  black pepper to taste

1. In a large nonreactive skillet combine the wine and the white portion of the scallion. Bring to a simmer.

2. Add the salmon fillets, cover, and simmer just until the fish is cooked through, about 8 minutes.

3. In a pan, sauté the fresh spinach with butter for 2 minutes. Distribute among 4 serving plates.

4. With a slotted spoon, remove the fish from the skillet, placing pieces atop the spinach on each serving plate. Tent with foil to keep warm.

5. Add the whipping cream to the skillet and bring to a simmer. Reduce the liquid until it coats the back of a spoon, about 6 minutes. Stir in the mustard and season to taste with salt and pepper.

6. To serve, spoon the sauce over the fish and sprinkle with the scallion tops.

## FUN FACT!

Breathtaking scenery abounds on cruises to Alaska. One port of call is a town called Skagway, a throwback to the Gold Rush days where residents have tried to preserve the original appearance of the town. An enjoyable way to view the scenery near Skagway is on the White Pass and Yukon Railway, a narrow gauge railroad that follows the Skagway River upstream past waterfalls and ice-packed gorges, and goes over a 1,000-foot-high wooden trestle bridge!

# braised yankee pot roast

YIELD: 8 SERVINGS

1 4-POUND (1.8 KG) BONELESS
BEEF POT ROAST, SUCH AS
BOTTOM ROUND RUMP ROAST

2 CLOVES GARLIC,
CUT INTO SLIVERS

SALT AND FRESHLY GROUND
BLACK PEPPER TO TASTE

1 TEASPOON DRIED THYME

1/4 CUP (60 ML) VEGETABLE OIL

1 CUP ROUGHLY CHOPPED
CARROTS

1 CUP ROUGHLY CHOPPED
CELERY

1 CUP ROUGHLY CHOPPED
ONION

1 CUP ROUGHLY CHOPPED LEEKS

4 TABLESPOONS TOMATO PASTE

2 BAY LEAVES

1 CUP (250 ML) DRY RED WINE

3 CUPS (720 ML) BEEF STOCK

1/2 CUP MUSTARD

1. If it has not been done for you by the butcher, tie the roast until compact and evenly shaped by wrapping and looping some kitchen twine across the roast at 1- or 2-inch (2.5 to 5 cm) intervals and then once from end to end. Pat the meat with paper towels to dry it thoroughly. Make several shallow slits in the meat with a paring knife and insert the garlic slivers. Season with salt and pepper and sprinkle with the thyme.

2. In a heavy casserole large enough to hold the roast, heat the oil over high heat. Add the meat and brown thoroughly on all sides until deep mahogany in color, about 15 to 20 minutes total. Remove the meat to a platter and set aside.

3. Add the carrots, celery, onion, and leeks to the casserole. Sauté, stirring, until browned, about 10 minutes. Reduce the heat to medium and add the tomato paste and bay leaves. Cook, stirring, for 2 minutes. Add the wine, beef stock, and mustard and scrape up any browned bits from the bottom of the casserole, stirring to dissolve them.

4. Add the roast back to the casserole and cover the casserole with a lid. Bring to a slight simmer. Simmer, covered, very gently for 3 to 4 hours, until the juices run clear or only faint pink when the roast is pricked with a fork.

5. Transfer the roast to a warmed serving platter and tent with aluminum foil to keep warm. Skim the fat from the juices in the casserole. Transfer the defatted juices and vegetables to a blender and puree. Season with salt and pepper.

6. To serve, slice the roast into 1/8-inch-thick (3 mm) slices and spoon the gravy over the top.

Note: This pot roast is delicious served with braised carrots, asparagus, and mashed potatoes.

# linzer torte

YIELD: 10 TO 12 SERVINGS

2 CUPS (220 G) ALL-PURPOSE
   FLOUR

1 TEASPOON GROUND
   CINNAMON

1 TEASPOON BAKING POWDER

1/2 TEASPOON SALT

1/4 TEASPOON GROUND CLOVES

10 TABLESPOONS UNSALTED
   BUTTER, SOFTENED

3/4 CUP (170 G) GRANULATED
   SUGAR

2 LARGE EGGS

1 TEASPOON PURE VANILLA
   EXTRACT

1/2 CUP (85 G) GROUND
   ALMONDS

1 TABLESPOON WHOLE MILK

1/2 CUP RASPBERRY JAM

1 LARGE EGG LIGHTLY BEATEN
   WITH 1 TABLESPOON WATER

CONFECTIONERS' SUGAR FOR
   DUSTING

1. In a medium bowl, whisk the flour, cinnamon, baking powder, salt, and cloves. Set aside. In a large mixing bowl, combine the butter and sugar. With an electric mixer, beat until fluffy, about 3 minutes. Add the eggs one at a time, beating well after each addition. Add the vanilla and beat until well combined.

2. With the mixer on low speed, beat the flour mixture into the butter mixture until just combined. With a spoon, stir in the almonds and milk. Gather the mixture into a soft ball of dough and flatten into a disk. Cover with plastic wrap and refrigerate for at least 30 minutes.

3. Preheat the oven to 350°F (180°C). Break off two-thirds of the dough and press it into an ungreased 10-inch (25-cm) springform pan so it covers the bottom and goes 3/4 inch (1.5 cm) up the sides. With a spatula, spread the raspberry jam evenly over the dough in the pan.

4. Divide the remaining dough into 10 equal pieces. Using floured hands, roll each into a 10-inch (25-cm) rope. Arrange the ropes in a lattice design over the filling, trimming the ends to fit. Brush the lattice and the edge of the pastry with the egg wash.

5. Bake the torte for 40 to 45 minutes, or until the pastry is golden brown. Transfer the pan to a wire rack and let cool completely. Run a knife around the edge of the pan and remove the side of the pan. Place the torte on a serving plate and sprinkle confectioners' sugar through a sieve over the top.

**TIP**

# 1

On a large tray, scatter blue tortilla chips and nestle in a bowl of your favorite tomato-based salsa and another of sour cream.

**TIP**

# 2

Play patriotic music: George M. Cohan, World War II–era music collections, or contemporary songs about freedom and independence.

**TIP**

# 3

Decorate with patriotic colors: put red, white, and blue confetti on the tables and poke mini-flag toothpicks into the Firecracker Shrimp.

**TIP**

# 4

For outdoor lighting, use hurricane lamps and camp lanterns, and string red, white, and blue lights on tree trunks and the deck railing or awning.

**TIP**

# 5

For a centerpiece, fill white glass milk jugs with red and white carnations and blue irises.

**TIP**

# 6

If festivities include a bonfire, have long sticks, marshmallows, graham crackers, and chocolate bars on hand to make s'mores.

**TIP**

# 7

As dusk falls, light citronella candles. It will keep away some of the mosquitoes and provide romantic and flattering light.

**TIP**

# 8

Make a sheet cake and ice it to resemble the American flag. Place mini red, white, and blue pinwheels on the cake.

# Fourth of July

Most days of the year, we take so many of the freedoms we have as Americans for granted. There is one day, however, dedicated to celebrating the freedoms we enjoy all year long: Independence Day.

The Declaration of Independence, drafted by Thomas Jefferson, was actually signed in August 1776, after it met with widespread public approval and even jubilation. The first official Independence Day celebration took place on July 4, 1777. By the 1800s many of the traditions we still follow—picnics, parades, and fireworks—were already established as the best ways to celebrate the birthday of the United States. Independence day is not some historical relic, though. It is the day to contemplate and celebrate the freedoms and pleasures we enjoy today.

The timing is perfect. It's summer and almost everyone gets to enjoy the day off. In between the parades in the morning and spectacular fireworks at night, you can throw your most memorable party of the summer.

The Fourth of July is a day for unbridled flag-waving patriotism and optimism about the coming year. It should be celebrated with a bang. This menu is pure fun. Set aside standbys such as hamburgers and hot dogs and try more flavorful examples of great American cooking: Firecracker Shrimp, refreshing Chilled Washington Apple Soup, and Baby Back Ribs. On the side, add traditional favorites such as coleslaw, corn on the cob, potato or pasta salad, and baked beans. For dessert, nothing will do but the quintessential icon of American desserts: Mom's Old Fashioned Apple Pie.

# firecracker shrimp

2 POUNDS (1 KG) JUMBO SHRIMP

1 CUP (250 ML) DRY WHITE WINE

1 TEASPOON MUSTARD SEEDS

1/2 TEASPOON CRUSHED RED PEPPER, PLUS EXTRA AS NEEDED

2 BAY LEAVES

1/2 LEMON

6 TABLESPOONS CHOPPED FRESH BASIL

2 TABLESPOONS CHOPPED FRESH ROSEMARY

1 TABLESPOON CHOPPED FRESH THYME

3 CLOVES GARLIC, MINCED

1 1/2 TABLESPOONS HERB-FLAVORED MUSTARD

5 TABLESPOONS FRESH LEMON JUICE

1 CUP (250 ML) EXTRA VIRGIN OLIVE OIL

SALT AND FRESHLY GROUND BLACK PEPPER TO TASTE

1 SMALL RED BELL PEPPER, CORED, SEEDED, AND DICED

1 SMALL YELLOW BELL PEPPER, CORED, SEEDED, AND DICED

**1.** Pull the legs off the shrimp and peel away most of the shell, leaving only the tail shell intact. With a paring knife, devein the shrimp by cutting down the back of the shrimp and washing out the intestinal vein just below the surface.

**2.** In a large nonreactive saucepan, combine the wine, mustard seeds, crushed red pepper, bay leaves, and lemon half. Add enough water to fill the pan three-fourths full. Bring to a boil over high heat and add the shrimp. Cook, stirring, until the shrimp are opaque in the center, about 3 to 4 minutes. Drain in a colander and let cool.

**3.** In a large bowl, combine the basil, rosemary, thyme, garlic, mustard, and lemon juice. Slowly whisk in the oil. Season with salt and pepper. Add crushed red pepper if desired.

**4.** Stir in the bell peppers and the shrimp. Cover and refrigerate for at least 3 hours. Before serving, bring to room temperature. Serve with crusty sourdough bread.

# chilled washington apple soup

6 CUPS (1.5 L) WATER

JUICE OF 2 LEMONS

4 TABLESPOONS GRANULATED
SUGAR

$1/2$ TEASPOON GROUND
CINNAMON, PLUS EXTRA
FOR GARNISH

18 GOLDEN DELICIOUS
APPLES, PEELED, CORED,
AND ROUGHLY DICED

4 CUPS (560 G) VANILLA
ICE CREAM

**1.** In a large nonreactive saucepan, combine all the ingredients except the ice cream. Bring the mixture to a boil. Reduce the heat and simmer, covered, until the apples are soft.

**2.** Transfer the soup in batches to a blender and purée until smooth. Strain the soup through a fine sieve into a bowl. Let cool to room temperature. Cover and refrigerate until cold, about 4 hours. To serve, stir in the ice cream and divide the soup among chilled soup bowls. Sprinkle with cinnamon and serve immediately.

## FUN FACT!

When spending the Fourth of July aboard the ships—going to exciting locations in the Bahamas, Hawaii, Alaska, or Europe—expect to enjoy a Red, White, and Blue party under the stars, a delicious All-American Adventure Dinner, as well as activities such as face painting for the kids, a special pool party for teens only, and Independence Day Arts & Crafts.

FOURTH OF JULY

# baby back ribs

YIELD: 4 SERVINGS

## Dry Rub

8 TABLESPOONS TIGHTLY
PACKED LIGHT BROWN SUGAR

3 TABLESPOONS KOSHER SALT

1 TABLESPOON CHILI POWDER

1/2 TEASPOON FRESHLY GROUND
BLACK PEPPER

1/2 TEASPOON CAYENNE PEPPER

1/2 TEASPOON OLD BAY
SEASONING

1/2 TEASPOON DRIED THYME

1/2 TEASPOON ONION POWDER

Whisk all the ingredients
together in a bowl until
combined. Store in a tightly
sealed glass jar until ready
to use.

## Baby Back Ribs

2 WHOLE SLABS PORK BABY BACK RIBS

1 CUP (250 ML) DRY WHITE WINE

2 TABLESPOONS WHITE WINE VINEGAR

2 TABLESPOONS WORCESTERSHIRE SAUCE

1 TABLESPOON HONEY

2 CLOVES GARLIC, CHOPPED

1. Place each slab of ribs on a piece of heavy-duty aluminum foil, shiny side down. Sprinkle each side generously with the dry rub, then pat it into the meat. Wrap the ribs in the foil and refrigerate for at least 1 hour.

2. Preheat the oven to 250°F (130°C). In a microwavable container, combine all the remaining ingredients and microwave on high for 1 minute. Transfer the wrapped ribs to a baking sheet. Open one end of the foil packet on each slab and pour in half of the braising liquid. Tilt the baking sheet to equally distribute the braising liquid.

3. Reseal the foil packets securely and bake the ribs in the oven for 2 1/2 hours. Remove from the oven and carefully pour the braising liquid into a medium saucepan. Bring to a simmer and reduce by half or until thick and syrupy.

4. To serve, brush the glaze onto the ribs. Place under the broiler just until the glaze caramelizes lightly. Slice each slab into 2 rib-bone portions. Pour the remaining hot glaze into a large bowl and toss the rib portions in the glaze. Transfer to a warmed platter and serve immediately.

# sitka slaw

## Dressing

2 TABLESPOONS SUNFLOWER OIL

1 TABLESPOON ALL-PURPOSE
FLOUR

1 TEASPOON DRY MUSTARD

1/2 CUP (125 ML) WATER

2 TEASPOONS WHITE WINE
VINEGAR

1 LARGE EGG, LIGHTLY BEATEN

SALT AND FRESHLY GROUND
BLACK PEPPER TO TASTE

PINCH OF CAYENNE PEPPER

PINCH OF GRANULATED SUGAR

In a nonreactive saucepan,
combine the oil, flour, and
mustard. Slowly whisk in the
remaining ingredients. Place
the pan over very low heat
and cook, stirring constantly,
until thickened. (Do not let
the mixture come to a simmer or boil.) Remove from
the heat and let cool slightly.

## To Assemble

1 POUND (450 G) GREEN CABBAGE, SHREDDED

2 MEDIUM CARROTS, COARSELY GRATED

5 STALKS CELERY, SLICED

SALT AND FRESHLY GROUND BLACK PEPPER TO TASTE

2 TABLESPOONS CHOPPED FRESH PARSLEY

In a bowl, combine the cabbage, carrots, and celery. Pour
the dressing over the salad and toss to coat. Season with
salt and pepper. Cover and refrigerate until cold. To serve,
sprinkle with parsley.

# strawberry lemonade

### YIELD: 8 SERVINGS

4 CUPS (1 L) WATER

1 1/2 CUPS (340 G) GRANULATED SUGAR

6 CUPS FRESH (OR FROZEN) STRAWBERRIES

1 CUP (250 ML) FRESH LEMON JUICE

ICE CUBES AS NEEDED

**1.** In a medium saucepan, heat the water and sugar over low heat until the sugar is completely dissolved; let cool, cover and refrigerate until cold.

**2.** In a blender or food processor, purée the strawberries with the water/sugar mixture. Add the lemon juice and serve immediately over ice.

# star-spangled sangria

### YIELD: 8 SERVINGS

4 CUPS (1 L) DRY RED WINE

1 CUP (250 ML) MINERAL WATER

1 CUP (250 ML) GRENADINE

2 MEDIUM ORANGES, PEELED AND SECTIONED, WITH MEMBRANES REMOVED

3 MEDIUM APPLES, PEELED AND CHOPPED

In a large bowl or jug, combine all the ingredients. Cover and refrigerate for at least 6 hours before serving.

# mom's old-fashioned apple pie

## Pie dough

1³/4 CUPS (195 G)
ALL-PURPOSE FLOUR

3 TABLESPOONS
GRANULATED SUGAR

PINCH SALT

1/3 CUP (75 G) CHILLED LARD,
CUT INTO SMALL PIECES

6 TABLESPOONS CHILLED
UNSALTED BUTTER,
CUT INTO SMALL PIECES

3 TO 4 TABLESPOONS
ICE WATER

1. In a large bowl, combine the flour, sugar, and salt. Using your fingertips, a pastry blender, or 2 knives, work the lard and butter into the flour mixture until the mixture resembles coarse crumbs. (Alternatively, combine the ingredients in a food processor, using short pulses.)

2. With a fork, stir in the ice water, using only as much as needed to gather the mixture into a soft ball of dough. Cut the dough in half and flatten each half into a disk. Cover with plastic wrap and chill in the refrigerator for at least 1 hour.

## Filling

3 POUNDS (1.3 KG) MCINTOSH APPLES, PEELED,
CORED, AND SLICED INTO 1/2-INCH (1.25-CM) SLICES

1/2 CUP (115 G) GRANULATED SUGAR

1 TABLESPOON FRESH LEMON JUICE

2 TEASPOONS GROUND CINNAMON

1/2 TEASPOON FRESHLY GRATED NUTMEG

1/2 CUP (125 ML) HEAVY CREAM

1. Preheat the oven to 450°F (230°C). In a large bowl, combine all the ingredients. Toss to coat.

2. On a lightly floured surface, roll out 1 disk of dough into an 11-inch (27.5-cm) circle, making sure the circle is larger than the pie pan by at least an inch (2.5 cm).

3. Drape the dough over a rolling pin and fit it into a 9-inch (22.5-cm) deep-dish pie pan. Pour the apple filling into the dough-lined pan. Roll out the remaining dough and place it over the filling. Gather together the edges of the bottom and top crusts, trim them if necessary, and press them onto the rim of the pie pan. Crimp the edge with your fingers or press it with the tines of a fork.

4. Cut 4 steam vents into the top of the pie. Bake for 20 minutes. Reduce the heat to 375°F (190°C) and bake for 40 minutes more, or until the pastry is golden brown. Serve the pie warm and, if desired, top with vanilla ice cream and red, white, and blue sprinkles.

**Note:** To save time on this recipe, buy a pie crust.

## QUICK STRAWBERRY SHORTCAKE

If you want to have the fixings for this July 4 classic on hand, buy pre-made pound cake, make whipped cream, and slice up fresh strawberries.

FOURTH OF JULY

## TIP
### 1

Rent banquet tables and chairs, or try to borrow them from your local church, school, or community center.

## TIP
### 2

Ask a craft-making family member to create a large family tree on an oversized tablecloth (heavy muslin is ideal) using indelible marker.

## TIP
### 3

Have hurricane lamps or candles available on the tables to be lit when it gets dark.

## TIP
### 4

Set up a bar with assorted mixers and liquors, garnishes, and glassware. Put sodas and beer into a cooler filled with ice. Place wine bottles in a tub with ice.

## TIP
### 5

Set up a children's bar with assorted fruit juices, seltzer, ginger ale, cherries, and swizzle sticks—they'll have a great time serving themselves.

## TIP
### 6

Collect small bunches of wildflowers, tie them loosely with ribbon, and set them into a variety of empty bottles.

## TIP
### 7

In a guest book ask everyone to write updated contact information along with a family memory. Compile into a newsletter.

## TIP
### 8

Use cloth napkins—they are more environmentally sound and won't blow away. Purchase a mismatched flea market set.

# Royal Reunion

These days, getting the immediate family together for a meal can be hard enough to accomplish—forget about far-flung relatives. That's why planning family reunions every few years should be a priority. Without a coming together of the generations, family histories can be lost and children and grandchildren may never realize that they are part of a larger family network.

The family reunion shouldn't be a dreaded family obligation. Events like this are wonderful opportunities for family history to come alive—to pass down personal stories and learn about events and people connected to us. Naturally, I think reunions are so important that families should go all out and take a cruise together! Of course, this might not be feasible on an annual basis (you should still try it at least once!), so a marathon family picnic during the summer is a fine stand in.

More than with most other celebrations, a family reunion needs to be planned well in advance—I'd say no less than six months. Once you set the date, it will be up to the rest of the family to keep their schedules clear for it. After that, the rest is relatively easy. The menu provided here includes homey and delicious dishes like grilled strip steaks, potato salad, and meatloaf (just like foods you would get on a Family Reunion Cruise). You can coordinate with other family members to make favorites that will appeal to every generation.

# vegetable sauté

1 MEDIUM EGGPLANT, SLICED

1 MEDIUM ZUCCHINI, SLICED

1 TEASPOON SALT

2 TEASPOONS OLIVE OIL

2 MEDIUM GREEN BELL PEPPERS, CORED, SEEDED, AND SLICED

2 MEDIUM CARROTS, PEELED AND SLICED INTO 1/4-INCH (6 MM) ROUNDS

1 CUP CHERRY TOMATOES

FRESHLY GROUND BLACK PEPPER TO TASTE

GROUND CINNAMON TO TASTE

1 TABLESPOON FINELY CHOPPED FRESH PARSLEY

1 TABLESPOON FINELY CHOPPED FRESH DILL

**1.** Slice the eggplant and zucchini into 1/4-inch-thick (6 mm) rounds; trim the ends. Sprinkle the slices with salt, lay them on paper towels, and let sit for 15 minutes. Rinse and pat dry with clean paper towels.

**2.** In a large skillet, heat the oil over medium heat. Add the eggplant and zucchini, and sauté until soft, about 2 to 3 minutes. Remove to a warmed serving dish. Add the carrots and sauté until tender. Then add the green peppers for another 2 minutes. Add back the lightly sautéed eggplants and zucchini, mixing with the rest of the vegetables. Lastly add the cherry tomatoes. Sauté the vegetables for a few minutes until tender. Season the vegetables with salt, pepper, and a dash of cinnamon. Sprinkle with parsley and dill.

# sovereign strip steaks
## with red pepper relish

6 LARGE RED BELL PEPPERS, CORED, SEEDED, AND CUT INTO JULIENNE STRIPS

PEELED ZEST FROM 4 LEMONS, CUT INTO JULIENNE STRIPS

1/2 CUP (125 ML) FRESH LEMON JUICE

2 MEDIUM YELLOW ONIONS, THINLY SLICED

8 CLOVES GARLIC, MINCED

2 CUPS (500 ML) RED WINE VINEGAR

2 CUPS (400 G) PACKED LIGHT BROWN SUGAR

1/4 CUP GROUND GINGER

1 TEASPOON CRUSHED RED PEPPER

PINCH CAYENNE PEPPER

SALT AND FRESHLY GROUND BLACK PEPPER TO TASTE

8 STRIP STEAKS, 6 TO 8 OUNCES (170 TO 225 G) EACH

**1.** In a large heavy saucepan, combine all the ingredients except the steaks. Cook over low heat, stirring constantly, for 2 hours.

**2.** Heat a charcoal or gas grill. Season the steaks with salt and pepper. Grill on both sides to the desired doneness. To serve, place the strip steaks on warmed plates and top with the red pepper relish. Serve immediately.

# shrimp potato salad

YIELD: 4 SERVINGS

1¼ POUNDS (700 G) SMALL
NEW POTATOES, 1 TO
2 INCHES (3 TO 5 CM) IN
DIAMETER

1 TABLESPOON VEGETABLE OIL

1 POUND (450 G) ROCK SHRIMP,
PEELED AND DEVEINED

SALT AND FRESHLY GROUND
BLACK PEPPER TO TASTE

1 HARD-COOKED LARGE EGG,
PEELED AND CHOPPED

3 TABLESPOONS PREPARED
MAYONNAISE

3 TABLESPOONS SOUR CREAM

¼ CUP FINELY CHOPPED DILL
PICKLE

1 TABLESPOON FINELY CHOPPED
SHALLOT

2 TABLESPOONS DIJON
MUSTARD

1 TABLESPOON FINELY CHOPPED
FRESH TARRAGON LEAVES OR
1 TEASPOON DRIED TARRAGON

1. In a large saucepan, cover the potatoes with water by 1 inch (3 cm) and simmer until just tender, about 15 to 20 minutes. Drain and let cool.

2. Meanwhile, heat the oil in a sauté pan over high heat. Add the shrimp and cook until firm and pink. Season with salt and pepper. Let cool.

3. In a large bowl, combine the remaining ingredients. Season with salt and pepper. Cut the potatoes into quarters and gently toss with the egg mixture. Add the shrimp and adjust the seasonings. Serve the potato salad chilled or at room temperature.

# majesty's mayfair meat loaf
## with creamy mushroom gravy
## and caramelized onions

YIELD: 8 TO 10 SERVINGS

### Meat Loaf

3 TABLESPOONS UNSALTED BUT-
TER

3/4 CUP FINELY CHOPPED ONION

1/4 CUP FINELY CHOPPED CELERY

1/4 CUP MINCED RED BELL
PEPPER

1/4 CUP MINCED GREEN BELL
PEPPER

2 TEASPOONS MINCED GARLIC

3 LARGE EGGS, WELL BEATEN

SALT TO TASTE

1 1/2 TEASPOONS FRESHLY
GROUND PEPPER

1/2 CUP (125 ML) KETCHUP

1/2 CUP (60 ML) HALF-AND-HALF

2 3/4 POUNDS (1.2 KG)
GROUND CHUCK

3/4 CUP FRESH BREAD CRUMBS

**1.** Preheat the oven to 375°F (190°C). In a heavy skillet; heat the butter over medium-high heat. Add the onion, celery, bell peppers, and garlic. Cook, stirring, until the moisture from the vegetables has evaporated.

**2.** Transfer the contents of the skillet to a bowl and let cool. Cover and refrigerate until completely cold.

**3.** In a large bowl, combine the eggs, salt, and pepper. Whisk until well combined. Stir in the ketchup and half-and-half.

**4.** Add the ground chuck and breadcrumbs to the egg mixture, stirring with a fork to incorporate. Add the chilled vegetables and gently mix them in with your hands (do not overmix).

**5.** With dampened hands, form the mixture into an oval that resembles a long loaf of bread. Transfer to a baking dish and bake for 1 hour. Serve with the mushroom gravy and the carmelized onions.

**Note:** Ground turkey meat can also be substituted for ground chuck.

ROYAL REUNION

## Creamy Mushroom Gravy

10 TABLESPOONS (150 G) UNSALTED BUTTER

1 POUND (454 G) WHITE MUSHROOMS, WIPED CLEAN, TRIMMED AND THINLY SLICED

4 TABLESPOONS ALL-PURPOSE FLOUR

5 TABLESPOONS FRESH LEMON JUICE

2 CUPS (500 ML) HEAVY CREAM

SALT AND PEPPER TO TASTE

CHOPPED FRESH PARSELY FOR GARNISH

In a large skillet, heat the butter over medium-high heat. Add the mushrooms and cook, stirring, until lightly browned, about 2 to 3 minutes. Add the flour and cook, stirring, for 2 minutes. Slowly stir in the lemon juice and cook until just heated through. Season with salt and pepper and serve immediately with the meat loaf. Garnish with chopped parsley.

## Caramelized Onions

2 TABLESPOONS OLIVE OIL

1 YELLOW ONION, THINLY SLICED

SALT AND FRESHY GROUND BLACK PEPPER TO TASTE

Heat 4 tablespoons of the oil in a medium saucepan over medium heat. Stir in the onions and sauté for 15 to 20 minutes, or until the onions are a dark golden brown. Serve with the meat loaf.

# bahamas banana blitz

## Pastry Cream

3 CUPS (750 ML) WHOLE MILK

1/2 VANILLA BEAN, SPLIT

1/2 CUP (115 G) GRANULATED SUGAR

3 LARGE EGG YOLKS

1/3 CUP CORNSTARCH

1. In a medium saucepan, bring the milk to a boil. Reduce the heat to low and use the tip of a blunt knife to scrape the vanilla bean seeds into the milk. Gently simmer, stirring occasionally, until the vanilla has infused the milk, about 15 minutes.

2. Meanwhile, in a mixing bowl, whisk the sugar and egg yolks until pale in color, about 2 minutes. Sift the cornstarch over the mixture and continue whisking until just incorporated. Slowly pour half of the vanilla-infused milk into the egg yolk mixture, gently whisking until well blended.

3. Prepare a large bowl of ice water. Return the egg yolk mixture to the saucepan and place over medium-low heat. Gently cook, stirring continually with a wooden spoon, until the mixture becomes thick and creamy, about 5 minutes. Immediately remove the mixture from the heat and strain through a fine sieve into a medium bowl. Place the bowl in the bowl of ice water to chill the mixture quickly.

4. When the pastry cream is cool, press a piece of plastic wrap onto the surface to prevent a skin from forming until ready to use.

## To Assemble

1/2 CUP (200 ML) HEAVY CREAM

1 TABLESPOON GRANULATED SUGAR

2 MEDIUM BANANAS, PEELED

1 BAKED 9-INCH (22.5-CM) PIE SHELL

12 MINT LEAVES FOR GARNISH

12 BANANA SLICES FOR GARNISH

WHIPPED CREAM FOR GARNISH

1. Place 1 cup pastry cream in a medium bowl. In a chilled mixing bowl, whip the heavy cream and sugar until stiff but still glossy. Add 1 cup whipped cream to the bowl of pastry cream, whisking until just combined. Spread enough pastry cream mixture into the baked pie shell to fill it by three-fourths.

2. Slice the bananas lengthwise and immediately arrange the slices in the cream-filled shell. Top with the remaining pastry cream mixture.

3. Cover the pie decoratively with the remaining whipped cream. Chill until ready to serve, or cut into 12 wedges and serve immediately. Before serving, garnish each piece with a rosette of whipped cream, banana slice, and mint leaf.

# rum rhapsody

1¹/₃ CUPS (325 ML) DARK RUM

1¹/₃ CUPS (325 ML) FROZEN PASSION FRUIT JUICE COCKTAIL CONCENTRATE, THAWED

1 CUP (250 ML) MANGO NECTAR

1 CUP (250 ML) GUAVA NECTAR

2 TABLESPOONS FRESH LIME JUICE, PLUS EXTRA AS NEEDED

4 CUPS ICE CUBES

6 FRESH PINEAPPLE WEDGES FOR GARNISH

**1.** In a large pitcher, mix the rum, passion fruit concentrate, mango nectar, guava nectar, and 2 tablespoons lime juice. Add more lime juice if desired.

**2.** Add the ice cubes and stir well to blend. Pour into 6 glasses. Garnish with the pineapple wedges and serve immediately.

## FUN FACT!

Eating is definitely a form of entertainment aboard Royal Caribbean ships such as *Rhapsody of the Seas*. It's possible, though perhaps not advisable, for guests to eat fifteen times a day! That's thanks to 24-hour in-room snack, lunch, and dinner service, plus alternative breakfast and lunch buffets in the Windjammer Café; regular dining room breakfasts, lunches, and dinners; midnight buffets; and pizzas in the solarium.

## TIP

# 1

Set up an outdoor bar area with fixings for favorite tropical drinks and garnishes. Slice lemons, limes, and pineapple.

## TIP

# 2

Line the bar with oversized, colorful glassware or plastic tumblers, and paper cocktail parasols and novelty swizzle sticks.

## TIP

# 3

Put several pitchers of water with lemon and lime slices on a table in the party area. Provide a supply of cups.

## TIP

# 4

Pipe Caribbean music out to your party area.

## TIP

# 5

String white lights or Chinese lanterns for evening lighting, and/or line the railing of the deck with votive candles.

## TIP

# 6

Upon arrival, give each woman a tropical flower to tuck behind her ear.

## TIP

# 7

Borrow lounge chairs to line around the pool, deck, or yard. Garden benches are also a good choice.

## TIP

# 8

Use starfish, sand dollars, seashells, and tropical flowers to create free-form centerpieces on dining tables.

# Deck &
# Pool Party

Vacations recharge and stimulate us, and enable us to leave our worries behind—at least for awhile. Unfortunately, many people don't get enough vacation time or procrastinate making plans. When I have summer parties (you don't need a deck or pool for it), I like to have the kinds of events that leave my friends feeling like they've had a mini getaway.

In the summer, my mind turns to tropical ports of call—to the bright colors of the Caribbean Islands and exotic flavors. With the right menu, a few simple decorations and, as we say in the hospitality business, "amenities," your yard, deck, or pool area can be transformed into a little slice of paradise.

This summer party menu starts with flavors from steamy vacation destinations: tropical fruit skewers with yogurt sauce; island-inspired Chilled Banana and Coconut Soup; a sunny, briny mediterranean Greek salad; delicious Lentil and Chickpea Burgers with a refreshing Cilantro Garlic Cream; and grilled Vegetable Brochettes. For dessert, make an all-American summer treat, Peach Cobbler with Vanilla Ice Cream.

Drinks should get particular attention during summer parties. I've included a recipe for Summer Slush—a fantastic refresher for a sweltering summer day. To punch up the rest of the bar, steer clear of the usual summer drinks like Gin and Tonic and Vodka Screwdrivers and mix it up a bit with pitchers of Daiquiris, Mai Tais, and other rum-spiked tropical drinks.

# maui melon medley
## with yogurt dipping sauce

YIELD: 6 SERVINGS

$^1/_2$ CUP (125 ML) MILK

1 CUP (250 G) PLAIN FAT-FREE YOGURT

1 TABLESPOON HONEY

2 TABLESPOONS LIGHTLY PACKED
LIGHT BROWN SUGAR

JUICE OF 1 LIME

$^1/_2$ CANTALOUPE, PEELED AND CUBED

$^1/_4$ WATERMELON, PEELED AND CUBED

$^1/_4$ HONEYDEW, PEELED AND CUBED

1 PINT STRAWBERRIES, STEMMED

3 TABLESPOONS FINELY CHOPPED FRESH MINT

6 6-INCH (15-CM) BAMBOO SKEWERS

1. In a medium bowl, whisk together the milk, yogurt, honey, brown sugar, and lime juice. Pour into a serving bowl.

2. In a large bowl, toss the fruit with the mint. Alternate pieces of cantaloupe, watermelon, honeydew, and strawberry on each skewer. (Each skewer should contain 2 pieces of each fruit.) Serve with the yogurt sauce on the side.

# chilled banana and coconut soup

YIELD: 5 SERVINGS

2 POUNDS (1 KG) RIPE BANANAS,
PEELED AND DICED

JUICE OF 1 LEMON

$^1/_2$ CUP (125 ML) PINEAPPLE JUICE

1 CUP (250 G) PLAIN YOGURT

2 CUPS (500 ML) CANNED COCONUT MILK

1 CUP VANILLA ICE CREAM

$^1/_4$ CUP (60 ML) DARK RUM OR TRIPLE SEC

$^1/_4$ CUP (20 G) SLICED ALMONDS

1. In a large nonreactive bowl, combine all the ingredients except the almonds. Ladle the mixture in batches into a blender and purée until smooth. Transfer the soup to a nonreactive bowl. Cover and refrigerate until cold.

2. Meanwhile, toast the almonds: In a dry skillet over high heat, toss or stir the almonds, taking care not to scorch them, until lightly browned. To serve, divide the cold soup among chilled soup bowls and garnish with the almonds.

# cyprus salad

## Lemon Dressing

1 TABLESPOON FRESH
LEMON JUICE

$^1/_4$ CUP (125 ML) EXTRA
VIRGIN OLIVE OIL

SALT AND FRESHLY GROUND
BLACK PEPPER TO TASTE

Place the lemon juice in a small nonreactive bowl. Slowly whisk in the oil. Season with salt and pepper. Cover and refrigerate until ready to use.

## To Assemble

$^1/_2$ HEAD ROMAINE LETTUCE, WASHED, DRIED, AND CHOPPED

1 CUP SHREDDED SPINACH LEAVES

3 MEDIUM TOMATOES, CUT INTO QUARTERS

$^1/_2$ CUCUMBER, PEELED, HALVED LENGTHWISE, SEEDED, AND SLICED

$^1/_2$ WHITE ONION, THINLY SLICED INTO RINGS

1 MEDIUM GREEN BELL PEPPER, CORED, SEEDED, AND SLICED

12 KALAMATA OLIVES, PITTED

6 OUNCES (170 G) FETA CHEESE, CUBED

1 TEASPOON CHOPPED FRESH OREGANO OR MARJORAM

In a large nonreactive serving bowl, combine the lettuce and spinach. Add the tomatoes, cucumber, onion, and bell pepper, and toss to combine. Arrange the olives and cheese on top and drizzle with the lemon dressing. Sprinkle with the oregano or marjoram and serve immediately.

# lentil and chickpea burgers
## with cilantro garlic cream

### Cilantro Garlic Cream

1/2 CUP (125 ML) SOUR CREAM

1/2 CUP (125 ML) HEAVY CREAM

1 CLOVE GARLIC, CRUSHED

2 TABLESPOONS CHOPPED FRESH CILANTRO

2 TABLESPOONS CHOPPED FRESH PARSLEY

Combine all the ingredients in a small bowl. Cover and refrigerate until ready to use.

### Lentil and Chickpea Burgers

1 CUP RED LENTILS, PICKED OVER FOR STONES AND RINSED

1 TABLESPOON VEGETABLE OIL

2 MEDIUM ONIONS, SLICED

1 TABLESPOON TANDOORI SEASONING (AVAILABLE FROM INDIAN GROCERY STORES)

1 15 1/2-OUNCE (439-G) CAN CHICKPEAS (OR GARBANZO BEANS), DRAINED

1 TABLESPOON GRATED FRESH GINGER

1 LARGE EGG

3 TABLESPOONS CHOPPED FRESH PARSLEY

2 TABLESPOONS CHOPPED FRESH CILANTRO

2 1/4 CUPS DRIED BREAD CRUMBS

SALT AND FRESHLY GROUND BLACK PEPPER TO TASTE

1. In a medium saucepan, combine the lentils and enough water to cover. Bring to a boil over medium-high heat. Reduce the heat to low and simmer, stirring occasionally, until tender, about 10 minutes. Drain and transfer to a bowl. Reserve.

2. In a skillet, heat the oil over medium heat. Add the onions and cook, stirring, until softened and translucent, about 8 minutes. Add the tandoori seasoning and stir until fragrant. Remove from the heat and let cool for 5 minutes.

3. In a food processor, combine the chickpeas, ginger, egg, onion mixture, and half the lentils. Purée until smooth. Transfer to a bowl and stir in the remaining lentils, parsley, cilantro, and bread crumbs. Season with salt and pepper and form the mixture into 6 patties. (If the mixture is too soft, refrigerate until firm.)

### To assemble

NONSTICK COOKING SPRAY

FLOUR FOR DUSTING

6 LETTUCE LEAVES

6 SLICES WHITE ONION

2 BEEFSTEAK TOMATOES, THINLY SLICED

6 HAMBURGER BUNS, TOASTED OR GRILLED

Heat a charcoal or gas grill to medium hot. Lightly coat the grill with nonstick cooking spray. Dredge the patties in a little flour and shake off the excess. Grill the patties, turning once, until browned, about 3 to 4 minutes on each side. Serve with toasted buns, lettuce, onion, tomato, and the cilantro garlic cream on the side.

# voyager vegetable brochettes

1 CUP (250 ML) EXTRA VIRGIN
OLIVE OIL

1/2 CUP (125 ML) DRY
WHITE WINE

4 CLOVES GARLIC, CRUSHED

1/2 CUP CHOPPED FRESH BASIL

1 TABLESPOON CHOPPED FRESH
ROSEMARY

1/2 TEASPOON SALT

1/2 TEASPOON FRESHLY GROUND
BLACK PEPPER

4 SMALL RED POTATOES,
SCRUBBED

4 BABY ARTICHOKES, STEMMED
AND TRIMMED

4 LARGE SHALLOTS, PEELED

4 SMALL ITALIAN EGGPLANTS

4 GREEN ITALIAN FRYING
PEPPERS

4 SMALL PLUM TOMATOES

2 SMALL HEADS RADICCHIO, CUT
IN HALF

8 LONG SPRIGS ROSEMARY,
PLUS EXTRA FOR GARNISH

NONSTICK COOKING SPRAY

1. In a nonreactive bowl, combine the oil, wine, garlic, basil, rosemary, salt, and pepper. Cover and let stand for 1 hour.

2. In a shallow roasting pan, evenly spread the potatoes, artichokes, shallots, and eggplants. In a large nonreactive bowl, combine the peppers, tomatoes, and radicchio. Pour 1 cup (250 ml) marinade over the vegetables in the roasting pan and the remaining marinade over the vegetables in the bowl. Let marinate, covered, for 4 hours, turning the vegetables occasionally.

3. Preheat the oven to 400°F (200°C). Uncover the roasting pan and bake the potato mixture for 35 minutes, basting frequently. Remove from the oven, let cool, and transfer to a large bowl. Add the vegetables from the other bowl and combine. Reserve the marinade.

4. Heat a charcoal or gas grill to medium hot. Thread the vegetables through their centers on thin 16- to-18-inch (40- to 45-cm) skewers, placing each type of vegetable on each skewer. Twist 1 or 2 sprigs rosemary between the vegetables along the length of each skewer.

5. Lightly coat the grill with nonstick cooking spray. Grill the vegetables about 6 inches (15 cm) from the heat, basting frequently with the marinade, until the peppers are blistering and the tomato skins pop, about 6 minutes on each side.

6. To serve, arrange the skewers on a large serving platter and garnish with the remaining rosemary.

# promenade peach cobbler
## with vanilla ice cream

YIELD: 8 SERVINGS

1/2 CUP (115 G) UNSALTED BUTTER, MELTED

4 CUPS FRESH PEACHES, PEELED, PITTED, AND SLICED OR ONE 1-POUND (450-G) CAN SLICED PEACHES

1 CUP (225 G) GRANULATED SUGAR

1/4 TEASPOON SALT

1 TEASPOON BAKING POWDER

1 CUP (110 G) ALL-PURPOSE FLOUR

1 TEASPOON GROUND CINNAMON

1/2 CUP (125 ML) WHOLE MILK

1 QUART VANILLA ICE CREAM

1. Preheat the oven to 350°F (175°C). Spread melted butter onto the bottom of a 9 x 13-inch (23 x 32-cm) baking pan.

2. Drain the peaches (if using canned) and place in the prepared pan.

3. In a mixing bowl, combine the sugar, salt, baking powder, flour, cinnamon, and milk. Spoon the batter over the peaches.

4. Bake for 45 minutes or until the top is brown and the peaches are bubbling.

5. Serve with vanilla ice cream.

# sunshine summer slush

YIELD: 6 SERVINGS

1 6-OUNCE (175-ML) CAN FROZEN LEMONADE CONCENTRATE

1 6-OUNCE (175 ML) CAN FROZEN ORANGE JUICE CONCENTRATE

1 CUP (250 ML) WATER

1 CUP ICE CUBES

1 CUP (250 ML) BOURBON OR RUM

Blend all the above in a blender until mixed well. To serve, spoon into glasses.

**FUN FACT!**

Every day is a deck and pool party aboard the ships. Whether enjoying the outdoor swimming pools and whirlpools, or the glass-enclosed indoor/outdoor solariums, there are plenty of places to relax, socialize, and enjoy the beautiful ocean views with a delicious tropical cocktail and snack in hand. After all, relaxing is an important activity in and of itself.

**TIP**
# 1

Be sure that you have two candlesticks on the table. It is customary to start the holiday with the blessing and lighting of two candles.

**TIP**
# 2

Appetizer ideas: Any pre-meal nibbles served should be light and sweet. Try cheese blintzes cut into thirds.

**TIP**
# 3

Use fine china, serving pieces, silverware, glassware, and linens for this holiday.

**TIP**
# 4

Say the *Kiddush* blessing over a special wine goblet— something reserved for use only during this holiday.

**TIP**
# 5

Put the challah bread on a beautiful tray and cover with a special embroidered or hand-painted cloth; give it a position of honor at the table before the blessing.

**TIP**
# 6

Use non-drip creamed honey. It's delicious, and will keep your table from getting messy. There are many wonderful varieties available.

**TIP**
# 7

Make a centerpiece of apples by mounding a beautiful pedestaled pie plate with different types of apples. It's stunning.

**TIP**
# 8

Pomegranates, which represent abundance, can also be used as decorations. Place clusters of them on the table.

# Rosh Hashanah

Rosh Hashanah celebrates the creation of the world. That has to be about the best reason to throw a party. While commonly referred to as the Jewish New Year (Rosh Hashanah translates to "head of the year"), that is just one important facet of the holiday. It is the beginning of a ten-day period known as the High Holy Days, which ends with Yom Kippur. Rosh Hashanah is also known as the Day of Judgment, in which the prior year's deeds are examined, and the Day of Remembrance, when the faithful contemplate their long history as a people.

Food is used to mark the joy and hopefulness of the holiday. The first night's meal begins with apples dipped in honey, which symbolizes the wish for blessings and a sweet year to come. Challah bread, a braided sweet loaf that is usually eaten on the Sabbath, is made in the shape of a crown for the Rosh Hashanah meal. It signifies the wish for a peaceful year to come. The challah loaf is blessed, broken, and then dipped in honey.

Carrots are another traditional ingredient in the Rosh Hashanah menu and represent a bounty of good things in the coming year. Carrots appear as an ingredient (both symbolic and flavorful) in many of these recipes. Carrot Tzimmes (meaning "mixture") is a dish commonly eaten for Rosh Hashanah. The carrots are traditionally cut in the shape of coins, a symbol for wealth during the year.

Because honey is such an integral part of the celebration, a honey cake is essential for the sweet blessings hoped for in the new year.

# mushroom and barley soup

YIELD: 8 SERVINGS

2 TABLESPOONS DRIED
PORCINI MUSHROOMS

2 TABLESPOONS MARGARINE

1 SPANISH ONION, THINLY
SLICED

2 STALKS CELERY, DICED

1 CARROT, PEELED AND SLICED

2 CLOVES GARLIC, CHOPPED

1/4 CUP CHOPPED PARSLEY

1 POUND (450 G) WHITE MUSH-
ROOMS, WIPED CLEAN AND
CHOPPED

1 TABLESPOON ALL-PURPOSE
FLOUR

2 QUARTS (2 L) BEEF STOCK
OR WATER

1 CUP WHOLE BARLEY

SALT AND FRESHLY GROUND
BLACK PEPPER TO TASTE

1. In a small bowl, soak the porcini mushrooms in enough hot water to cover for 30 minutes. Strain through a paper filter or cheesecloth and reserve the soaking liquid. Coarsely chop the porcini.

2. Heat the margarine in a heavy skillet. Add the onion, celery, carrot, garlic, 2 tablespoons parsley, the fresh mushrooms, and the porcini mushrooms. Cook, stirring, until the onion softens, about 5 minutes.

3. Reduce the heat and add the flour, stirring every 30 seconds, until the mixture thickens, about 5 minutes. Meanwhile, heat the beef stock or water in a soup pot over high heat.

4. When the stock begins to simmer, reduce the heat and begin to add the mushroom mixture, 1 cup at a time, stirring constantly. After all the mixture has been incorporated, increase the heat to high and add the reserved mushroom liquid and barley.

5. Simmer, covered but stirring occasionally, until the barley is tender and the soup is thickened, about 1 hour. Stir in the remaining 2 tablespoons parsley and season with salt and pepper.

# braised beef brisket
## with dried fruits, yams, and carrots

YIELD: 8 SERVINGS

3 TABLESPOONS
VEGETABLE OIL

3 MEDIUM ONIONS, CHOPPED

4 LARGE CLOVES GARLIC,
CHOPPED

1 TEASPOON PAPRIKA, PLUS
EXTRA FOR RUBBING

$^1/_2$ TEASPOON GROUND
ALLSPICE

$^1/_4$ TEASPOON CRUSHED
RED PEPPER

$3^1/_2$ CUPS (850 ML) BEEF STOCK
OR WATER

$1^1/_2$ CUPS (375 ML) DRY
RED WINE

3 BAY LEAVES

SALT TO TASTE

1 4-POUND (1.8 KG)
BONELESS FIRST-CUT
BEEF BRISKET

1 6-OUNCE (170 G) PACKAGE
DRIED APRICOTS

$1^1/_2$ CUPS PITTED PRUNES

3 POUNDS (1.4 KG) YAMS,
PEELED AND CUT INTO
$1^1/_2$-INCH (4-CM) PIECES

6 LARGE CARROTS, PEELED AND
CUT INTO $1^1/_2$-INCH
(4-CM) PIECES

MINCED FRESH PARSLEY
FOR GARNISH

1. Preheat the oven to 325°F (170°C). Heat the oil in a large flameproof casserole or Dutch oven over medium-high heat. Add the onions and garlic and cook, stirring frequently, until they begin to brown, about 15 minutes.

2. Add 1 teaspoon paprika, and the allspice and crushed red pepper; stir for 20 seconds. Add the beef stock, wine, and bay leaves. Boil for 10 minutes to allow the flavors to blend. Season with salt.

3. Sprinkle the brisket with paprika and rub it in. Add the brisket to the casserole, fat side up. Add the apricots and prunes. Cover and bake for $1^1/_2$ hours.

4. Add the yams and carrots to the casserole. Cover and bake for $2^1/_2$ hours longer, or until the brisket is very tender. Remove from the oven and let stand for 20 minutes.

5. Transfer the brisket to a cutting board and slice it thinly across the grain. Arrange the slices on a warmed platter. Surround the brisket with the fruit and vegetables. Remove bay leaves. Degrease the pan juices and spoon them over the meat. Garnish with parsley.

## FUN FACT!

Royal Culinary Collections is a product line of tasty dressings, vinegars, sauces, marinades, and spices that makes it easy for home cooks to create delicious meals. The line also makes it possible to replicate the flavors our guests experienced—or can experience—while dining aboard Royal Caribbean ships. Aside from making unique souvenirs and gifts, they bring back fond memories of cruising with Royal Caribbean International.

# zippy tzimmes

1 CUP (250 ML) CHICKEN STOCK

1/3 CUP (75 ML) FRESH ORANGE
JUICE

2 TABLESPOONS FRESH LEMON
JUICE

2 TABLESPOONS LIGHTLY
PACKED DARK BROWN SUGAR

3 TABLESPOONS HONEY

1/2 TEASPOON GROUND
CINNAMON

1/2 TEASPOON GROUND GINGER
OR 1 COIN-SIZE SLICE FRESH
GINGER, MINCED

1/2 TEASPOON SALT

PINCH FRESHLY GROUND BLACK
PEPPER

PINCH NUTMEG

2 TABLESPOONS MARGARINE,
PLUS EXTRA FOR GREASING

5 CARROTS, PEELED AND CUT
DIAGONALLY INTO 1-INCH
(2-CM) PIECES

3 SWEET POTATOES, PEELED
AND CUT INTO 1-INCH
(2-CM) PIECES

1 8-OUNCE (225-G) CAN
PINEAPPLE CHUNKS

1. Preheat the oven to 375°F (190°C). Lightly coat an 8 x 11-inch (20 x 28-cm) shallow baking dish with margarine.

2. In a saucepan, combine the chicken stock, orange juice, lemon juice, brown sugar, honey, cinnamon, ginger, salt, pepper, nutmeg, and margarine. Bring to a boil. Reduce the heat and simmer for 2 to 3 minutes.

3. Arrange the carrots, sweet potatoes, and pineapple in the prepared baking dish. Pour the hot stock mixture over the vegetables and fruit, turning them to coat.

4. Cover the dish with aluminum foil and bake for 1 hour, or until the potatoes are tender. Uncover and bake for 7 minutes longer, basting frequently, until the carrots and sweet potatoes are golden brown on top.

# apricot-pistachio honey cake

YIELD: 16 SERVINGS

NONSTICK COOKING SPRAY

3¹/₂ CUPS (390 G)
ALL-PURPOSE FLOUR

2 TEASPOONS BAKING
POWDER

1 TEASPOON BAKING SODA

1 TEASPOON GROUND
CINNAMON

¹/₂ TEASPOON GROUND
CARDAMOM

¹/₄ TEASPOON GROUND CLOVES

¹/₂ TEASPOON SALT

¹/₂ CUP (125 ML) BOILING
WATER

2 CUPS (500 ML) HONEY

¹/₄ CUP (60 ML) CANOLA OIL

1 TABLESPOON PLUS
1 TEASPOON FRESH
LEMON JUICE

GRATED ZEST OF 1 LEMON

3 LARGE EGGS

1 CUP (225 G) GRANULATED
SUGAR

1¹/₂ CUPS DRIED APRICOTS,
QUARTERED

1 CUP SHELLED PISTACHIOS,
ROUGHLY CHOPPED

1. Preheat the oven to 325°F (170°C). Line two 9 x 5-inch (23 x 13-cm) loaf pans with aluminum foil and lightly coat with nonstick spray.

2. In a medium bowl, combine the flour, baking powder, baking soda, spices, and salt. In another medium bowl, combine the boiling water and honey. Stir the oil, lemon juice, and zest into the honey mixture.

3. In the bowl of an electric mixer, beat the eggs and sugar until pale in color. With a rubber spatula, alternately fold the dry ingredients and honey mixture into the egg mixture, making 3 additions of dry ingredients and 2 additions of liquid. Fold in the apricots and pistachios.

4. Divide the batter between the prepared loaf pans. Place the pans on a baking sheet and bake the loaves for about 1 hour and 10 minutes, or until a skewer inserted in the center of each comes out clean.

5. Transfer the pans to a wire rack and let cool for 10 minutes. Unmold and let cool completely before slicing.

# challah bread

YIELD: 12 SERVINGS

1/4 CUP (55 G) GRANULATED
SUGAR

1/4 CUP (60 ML) CANOLA
OR VEGETABLE OIL, PLUS
EXTRA FOR GREASING

1 TEASPOON SALT

1 1/4 CUPS (210 ML) HOT WATER

1 PACKAGE ACTIVE DRY YEAST
(1/4 OUNCE / 7 G)

2 LARGE EGGS, AT ROOM
TEMPERATURE

2 TO 3 DROPS YELLOW
FOOD COLORING OR A
PINCH SAFFRON

5 CUPS (550 G) ALL-PURPOSE
FLOUR

1 LARGE EGG YOLK,
LIGHTLY BEATEN WITH
1 TABLESPOON WATER

POPPY SEEDS AND SESAME
SEEDS FOR SPRINKLING,
IF DESIRED

1. In a large bowl combine the sugar, oil, and salt. Stir in the hot water until the sugar is dissolved. Cool to lukewarm and add the yeast, stirring until dissolved. Add the eggs and food coloring or saffron and mix well.

2. Stir in 4 1/2 cups flour to make a soft dough. Sprinkle the remaining 1/2 cup flour on a work surface and scrape the dough out onto it. Knead until smooth and elastic, about 5 minutes, adding a little more flour if needed.

3. Rinse, dry, and lightly oil the bread bowl. Transfer the dough to the bowl and turn to coat with the oil. Cover with a clean kitchen towel and let rise in a warm place for 1 1/2 hours.

4. Lightly oil a large baking sheet. Punch down the dough. If you're going to make 2 smaller loaves, divide the dough in half and work with 1 half at a time.

5. Divide the dough into 4 equal sections. Roll 3 sections into ropes about 16 to 18 inches (40 to 46 cm) long. Braid the ropes starting in the middle and working to the ends. After each side is done, tuck under the tips.

6. Divide the fourth section into 3 parts. Roll into ropes about 8 inches (20 cm) long and braid as above.

7. Center the small braid lengthwise on top of the larger braid. Pinch the ends of the small braid down onto the larger. Transfer the bread to the prepared baking sheet, cover with a clean kitchen towel, and let rise for 1 hour.

8. Preheat the oven to 350°F (180°C). Brush the bread(s) evenly with the egg wash. Sprinkle with the seeds, if using, and bake for 30 to 35 minutes, until the loaves are dark brown and sound hollow when tapped. (If baking 2 loaves, place a rack in the middle and a rack in the upper third of the oven, switching the baking sheets halfway through.) Transfer to a rack to cool.

Note: It is usual for Rosh Hashanah challah to be made into a crown, not the more typical long braided loaf.

## TIP 1

Make sure that you set up your bar with top-shelf brands since cocktails are definitely the stars at this party.

## TIP 2

Focus the evening on variations of one cocktail such as the Martini, Manhattan, or Cosmopolitan and whip up pitchers of each.

## TIP 3

Place appetizers on tables all around the party area to keep guests from clustering in one place.

## TIP 4

Create a club atmosphere with some soft-colored light bulbs. Avoid overhead lights unless they are on dimmer switches. Put tea lights or votives on each table.

## TIP 5

When you visit flea markets or antique stores, watch for antique martini shakers, glass coasters, ice buckets, and the like to put into your cocktail party collection.

## TIP 6

Play lounge music: Chet Baker, Ella Fitzgerald, Frank Sinatra, Nancy Wilson, Etta James, and Duke Ellington are good choices.

## TIP 7

Use glass, not plastic! If you don't have retro glassware it's available at housewares stores and is a fun investment.

## TIP 8

Remove most of the chairs in your entertaining area to encourage mingling; bring in extra end tables for drinks and food.

# Cocktail Party

Cocktail parties are the easiest events in which to enjoy your own party. Most everything can be done in advance, and you don't have to leave the festivities to get dinner on the table. Perhaps best of all, you don't need any specific reason to hold a cocktail party—having fun is the whole point.

The concept of the cocktail party was born in 1920 when the 18th amendment ushered in the era of prohibition. A popular form of weeknight and weekend entertainment—going out for a drink—vanished overnight. Speakeasies filled part of the gap, serving up smuggled, illegal alcohol; the rest was filled by private parties held in homes where mixed drinks were made with homemade bathtub gin.

The height of cocktail party popularity was during the 1950s when Hollywood's Rat Pack brought an unprecedented glamour and sophistication to this form of entertaining. Indeed, swank cocktail parties created an entire entertaining culture that included hipsters, business people, and housewives alike. During the 1960s and '70s, chic cocktail parties gave way to more casual forms of entertaining, and the 1980s saw the decade of "cocooning." Home was a place for couch potatoes and the VCR, not parties, and entertainment came in the form of eating out. During the 1990s, however, the boom in gourmet ingredients, high-end cooking equipment, and designer kitchens gave rise to a resurgence in the notion of chic home entertaining. By the end of the decade it was clear that the cocktail party was back in fashion.

Holiday entertaining includes family members of all ages but the cocktail party is, clearly, the exclusive province of adults. A glamorous ambiance can be created with the menu choices, music, and lighting—and by inviting guests to dress up for the occasion. It's fun for everyone!

# viking vegetable spring rolls
## with spicy-sweet peanut dipping sauce

### Peanut Dipping Sauce

1/4 CUP (60 ML) PEANUT OIL

1 CUP FINELY CHOPPED ONION

1/4 CUP MINCED FRESH GINGER

3 TABLESPOONS MINCED GARLIC

3 SMALL RED HOT CHILE PEPPERS, SEEDED AND FINELY CHOPPED

4 TABLESPOONS GRANULATED SUGAR

1/3 CUP (75 ML) SOY SAUCE

3 TABLESPOONS FRESH LIME JUICE

1 CUP CHUNKY PEANUT BUTTER

1/2 CUP (125 ML) UNSWEETENED CANNED COCONUT MILK, PLUS EXTRA AS NEEDED

1/4 CUP CHOPPED FRESH CILANTRO

1. In a skillet, heat the oil over medium heat. Add the onion, ginger, garlic, and chile peppers. Cook, stirring, until the vegetables are softened and the onion is barely browned, about 8 to 10 minutes.

2. Meanwhile, combine the sugar, soy sauce, and lime juice, and stir to dissolve the sugar. When the onion is browned, add the sugar mixture, peanut butter, and coconut milk. Cook, stirring constantly, for 5 minutes. Add more coconut milk to thin the sauce if necessary. Remove from the heat and let cool. Stir in the cilantro and reserve.

### Spring Rolls

1 QUART (1 L) PEANUT OIL FOR SAUTÉING AND FRYING

1 CLOVE GARLIC, CRUSHED

5 WHITE MUSHROOMS, WIPED CLEAN AND CHOPPED

2 SCALLIONS, CHOPPED

1/4 CUP CHOPPED RED BELL PEPPER

2 CUPS SHREDDED CHINESE CABBAGE

1/4 CUP (60 ML) CHICKEN STOCK

2 TEASPOONS SOY SAUCE

2 TEASPOONS WATER

1 TABLESPOON CORNSTARCH

1 EGG WHITE, BEATEN

6 LARGE RICE PAPER SPRING ROLL SKINS (AVAILABLE AT ASIAN GROCERIES OR GOURMET FOOD STORES)

6 PARSLEY SPRIGS, WASHED AND DRIED

1. In a skillet, heat 1 teaspoon of oil over medium heat. Add the garlic and cook for 30 seconds. Add the mushrooms and cook, stirring, for 2 minutes. Stir in the scallions, bell pepper, and cabbage. Cook, covered, until the cabbage is wilted, about 10 minutes.

2. Meanwhile, whisk the chicken stock, soy sauce, water, and cornstarch. When the cabbage is wilted, add the cornstarch mixture and cook, stirring constantly, for 2 minutes. Remove from the heat and keep warm.

3. Fill a wide shallow bowl or cake pan with warm water and spread out several dry kitchen towels nearby. Immerse a sheet of rice paper into the warm water. Quickly withdraw it and lay it flat on a kitchen towel. Repeat with the remaining rice papers, without letting them touch each other on the kitchen towels. The rice papers will become pliable within seconds.

4. Divide the vegetable mixture into 6 portions and place a portion on the bottom third of each sheet of rice paper. Brush the outer edge of the paper with the egg white. This will help keep the spring roll together. Fold the sides of the rice paper in and roll up each like a cylinder.

5. Preheat the oven to 200°F (95°C) and place a baking sheet in it. Pour 1 to 1¹/₂ inches (2.5-3.75 cm) peanut oil into a large cast iron skillet or heavy pan. Heat to 325°F (160°C). (A small piece of bread dropped into the oil should float up to the surface almost immediately and brown within 1 minute if it is hot enough.)

6. Working in batches, fry 2 rolls at a time for 10 to 12 minutes, turning often, until golden and crisp (do not let the rolls touch or they will stick together). Using tongs, remove the rolls from the oil and transfer to a plate lined with paper towels to drain. Transfer the rolls to the baking sheet in the oven to keep warm while frying the remaining rolls.

7. To serve this dish, cut each roll in half on the bias. Lay one half down on the plate, with the other leaning against it. Garnish with a parsley sprig and serve with the peanut sauce on the side.

# cucumber yogurt dip
## with tortilla chips

YIELD: 4 SERVINGS

2 8-OUNCE (250-G)
CONTAINERS PLAIN YOGURT

1 POUND (450 G) CUCUMBER,
PEELED, SEEDED, AND FINELY
CHOPPED

2 TEASPOONS FINELY CHOPPED
FRESH DILL, PLUS WHOLE
SPRIGS FOR GARNISH

3 CLOVES GARLIC, MINCED

1 TABLESPOON EXTRA
VIRGIN OLIVE OIL

1 TABLESPOON FRESH
LEMON JUICE

SALT AND FRESHLY GROUND
WHITE PEPPER TO TASTE

TORTILLA CHIPS (ALSO PITA
BREAD WEDGES)

1. Spoon the yogurt into a fine sieve placed over a bowl. Cover with plastic wrap and let drain in the refrigerator for 6 hours.

2. Place the cucumber in a clean kitchen towel and twist to remove excess moisture. Transfer to a nonreactive bowl and add the drained yogurt, chopped dill, garlic, oil, and lemon juice. Whisk to combine. Season with salt and white pepper.

3. Cover the bowl with plastic wrap and refrigerate for at least 2 hours and up to 8 hours to allow the flavors to blend. To serve, stir the dip, garnish with the dill sprigs, and accompany it with the pita wedges.

# crispy vegetable strudel

YIELD: 4 TO 6 SERVINGS

BUTTER OR NONSTICK COOKING
  SPRAY FOR GREASING

12 LARGE SPINACH LEAVES,
  TOUGH STEMS REMOVED

2 TABLESPOONS EXTRA VIRGIN
  OLIVE OIL

1 MEDIUM ONION,
  FINELY SLICED

1 MEDIUM RED BELL PEPPER,
  CORED, SEEDED, AND CUT
  INTO STRIPS

1 MEDIUM GREEN BELL PEPPER,
  CORED, SEEDED, AND CUT
  INTO STRIPS

2 MEDIUM ZUCCHINI, SLICED
  INTO ROUNDS

2 MEDIUM ITALIAN EGGPLANTS,
  CUT IN HALF LENGTHWISE AND
  SLICED

SALT AND FRESHLY GROUND
  BLACK PEPPER TO TASTE

6 SHEETS PHYLLO DOUGH
  (18 X 14 INCHES)
  (46 X 36 CM)

1/3 CUP CHIFFONADE OF
  FRESH BASIL

1/2 CUP GRATED CHEDDAR
  CHEESE

3 TABLESPOONS UNSALTED
  BUTTER, MELTED

2 TABLESPOONS SESAME SEEDS

1. Preheat the oven to 415°F (210°C). Lightly coat a baking sheet with butter or nonstick cooking spray.

2. Wash the spinach leaves thoroughly and steam them in a covered saucepan on the stove or in the microwave oven until just wilted. Squeeze out any excess moisture and spread the leaves out on paper towels to dry.

3. In a skillet, heat the oil over medium heat. Add the onion and cook, stirring, for 3 minutes. Add the bell peppers, zucchini, and eggplants. Cook, stirring, until the vegetables soften, about 5 minutes more. Season with salt and pepper. Remove from the heat and let cool.

4. Lay 1 sheet of phyllo on a work surface. (Keep the remaining phyllo covered with plastic wrap and a damp kitchen towel.) With a pastry brush, brush the phyllo sheet lightly with some melted butter. Top with a second sheet of phyllo. Repeat with the remaining phyllo, brushing with butter between each layer, until you have a stack.

5. Arrange the spinach, cooked vegetables, basil, and cheese along 1 long edge of the phyllo, about 2 inches (5 cm) from the short edge on each side. Roll up the phyllo into a cylinder, folding the short edges in to make a tight seal.

6. Place the strudel seam-side down on the prepared baking sheet. Brush with melted butter and sprinkle with the sesame seeds. Bake for 25 minutes, or until golden brown and crisp. Slice and serve immediately.

# kauai crudités cocktail
## with garlic and ginger soy dip

YIELD: 4 SERVINGS

### Crudités

4 CARROTS, PEELED AND CUT INTO STRIPS

1/2 BUNCH BROCCOLI, BROKEN INTO FLORETS

1/2 SMALL CAULIFLOWER, BROKEN INTO FLORETS

1 MEDIUM CUCUMBER, PEELED, SEEDED, AND CUT INTO STRIPS

2 RED OR YELLOW BELL PEPPERS, CORED, SEEDED, AND CUT INTO STRIPS

4 STALKS CELERY, TRIMMED AND CUT INTO STRIPS

4 CHERRY TOMATOES, STEMS LEFT ON

4 SCALLIONS, TRIMMED

4 RADISHES, TRIMMED

After rinsing and cutting the vegetables, sprinkle them with water, cover them with plastic wrap, and refrigerate until ready to use. If you wish to shape the radishes into flowers, make 4 petal-like cuts into each radish with a paring knife and put them in a bowl with cold water to cover. In about 30 minutes the "petals" will open.

### Garlic and Ginger Soy Dip

1/2 CUP (125 ML) PREPARED MAYONNAISE

1/4 CUP (60 ML) SOUR CREAM

3 TABLESPOONS SOY SAUCE

2 TABLESPOONS CHOPPED FRESH BASIL

1 TABLESPOON CHOPPED FRESH CILANTRO

1 TABLESPOON ORIENTAL SESAME OIL

1 TABLESPOON FINELY MINCED GARLIC

1 TABLESPOON RICE WINE VINEGAR

1 TEASPOON MINCED PEELED FRESH GINGER

1 TEASPOON GRANULATED SUGAR

1/2 TEASPOON DRY MUSTARD

PINCH CAYENNE PEPPER

SALT AND FRESHLY GROUND BLACK PEPPER TO TASTE

Combine all the ingredients except for the salt and pepper in a nonreactive bowl. Whisk to blend. Season with salt and pepper. Cover and refrigerate for at least 30 minutes to allow the flavors to develop.

### To Assemble

4 LEAVES RED LEAF LETTUCE

1 SMALL BUNCH FRISÉE LETTUCE

8 FRESH CHIVES

4 SPRIGS FRESH MINT

Divide the crudités, lettuces, and chives among 4 stylish drink glasses, arranging them as if you were arranging flowers in vases. Divide the dip among 4 other drink glasses and garnish with the mint sprigs. Serve a glass of vegetables and a glass of dip per person.

Note: The vegetables listed are available in most supermarkets and are good starter suggestions. However, there are many exciting choices when it comes to crudités, including sugar snap peas, Belgian endive leaves, jicama sticks, and daikon radish sticks. Use your imagination, just make sure that the vegetables are fresh and at peak flavor.

# high society satés
## with hoisin dipping sauce

4 LARGE CLOVES GARLIC,
THINLY SLICED

2 TABLESPOONS FINELY
GRATED FRESH GINGER

1/2 CUP (125 ML) FRESH LIME
JUICE, OR TO TASTE

SALT AND FRESHLY GROUND
BLACK PEPPER TO TASTE

1 POUND (450 G) SKIRT STEAK

1/2 CUP (125 ML) HOISIN SAUCE
(AVAILABLE AT ASIAN
GROCERIES OR GOURMET
FOOD STORES)

2 TABLESPOONS KETCHUP

32 BAMBOO SKEWERS,
SOAKED IN WARM WATER
FOR 20 MINUTES

NONSTICK COOKING SPRAY

LIME WEDGES FOR GARNISH

1. Heat a charcoal grill. In a shallow glass dish, combine the garlic, ginger, and 1/4 cup lime juice. Season marinade with salt and pepper.

2. Holding a knife at a 45-degree angle, cut the steak crosswise into 1/4-inch (.5-cm) thick slices. Add to the marinade and toss to coat well. Let marinate at room temperature for 10 minutes.

3. In a small bowl whisk the hoisin sauce and ketchup. Season to taste with the remaining lime juice, salt, and pepper.

4. Drain the skewers. Weave a skewer lengthwise through each slice of steak, stretching the slice on the skewer to flatten it. Transfer satés to a plate and season with salt and pepper.

5. Spray the grill with nonstick cooking spray. Grill the satés about 5 to 6 inches (13 to 15 cm) over glowing coals for 30 seconds to 1 minute on each side for medium-rare. Transfer to a platter and serve hoisin sauce and lime wedges alongside.

### FUN FACT!

On a typical seven-night Caribbean cruise aboard the super-huge *Explorer of the Seas*, more than three thousand guests enjoy: 1,600 pounds of ribs, 1.5 tons of chicken, 3,000 lobster tails, 500 pounds of fresh salmon, 1,500 pounds of shrimp, as well as 5,000 bottles of wine, 20,000 cans of beer, and 1,000 bottles of liquor!

# strawberries romanoff

1¹/₂ QUARTS FRESH STRAWBERRIES, RINSED, TRIMMED, AND HALVED

¹/₂ CUP (125 ML) GRAND MARNIER

1 TABLESPOON GRANULATED SUGAR

1 CUP (250 ML) HEAVY CREAM

1 PINT VANILLA ICE CREAM, SLIGHTLY DEFROSTED

¹/₄ CUP (60 ML) FRESH LEMON JUICE

4 MINT SPRIGS

1. In a nonreactive bowl, combine the strawberries, 2 tablespoons Grand Marnier, and sugar. Cover and refrigerate.

2. In a chilled mixing bowl, whip the heavy cream until it forms stiff peaks. In another chilled bowl, beat the vanilla ice cream with a wooden spoon. Fold in the whipped cream, lemon juice, and remaining Grand Marnier; blend until it is smooth.

3. Arrange some of the strawberries on the bottom of 4 parfait glasses, followed by some of the whipped ice cream. Top with more strawberries and ice cream and garnish each with a mint sprig. Serve at once.

Note: If you do not have parfait glasses, cereal bowls make a fine substitute.

## FUN FACT!

In addition to all of the meat, fish, poultry—and alcohol—consumed on *Explorer of the Seas*, its three thousand plus guests also consume 700 gallons of ice cream, 3,000 pounds of fresh fruit, and 500 pounds of cheese over the week-long cruise.

**TIP 1**

Pick autumn colors to decorate your table—golds, sienna, pumpkin, burgundy, deep sage, and antique white.

**TIP 2**

Use a mismatched collection of tableware for a chic look if you don't have formal china.

**TIP 3**

Line your table with mirrored tiles and set mini pumpkins, gourds, and squash, interspersed with votive candles, on them.

**TIP 4**

A few minutes before you put a hot side dish onto a serving plate, run hot water over it for a minute or two so your hot food doesn't go onto an ice cold plate.

**TIP 5**

Set up a dessert buffet before dinner with the sweet treats, servers, dessert plates, small napkins, coffee cups, saucers, spoons, dessert forks, cinnamon, and sugar.

**TIP 6**

Immediately after dinner, whip cream and put it on the dessert buffet along with hot coffee and tea, and cream.

**TIP 7**

Another centerpiece idea: take a large crystal punch bowl, fill with water, and set cranberries and non-scented floating candles in it.

**TIP 8**

Lay out the serving dishes you will need. Use sticky flags to mark which serving pieces will be used for each dish.

# Thanksgiving

Ask most Americans what their favorite holiday is and chances are they will say Thanksgiving; if the person enjoys cooking, the chances are even greater, because Thanksgiving is the ultimate holiday for people who love to cook. The planning of the menu, the shopping for specialty items, the selection of the turkey, the chopping and stirring and basting, and the final ceremony of the meal itself—all take on a special significance unmatched at any other time of the year.

The first Thanksgiving is the most famous meal in American history. In 1863, President Abraham Lincoln established it as a national day of hope, thanks, and forgiveness. Thanksgiving remains a day devoted to family and friends, and to remembrance. Over the years, Americans have added their own meanings and rituals to the historical foundation of this great holiday. Thanksgiving celebrations today can feature fish, beef, or purely vegetarian cuisine, but the traditional Thanksgiving meal revolves around the turkey and it is the centerpiece of the menu I've created here.

Of course, a turkey can be prepared in any number of ways—more Americans are deep frying and even barbecuing the big bird—but the most customary method is roasting. From the time it is put into the oven in the morning, through the mouth-watering roasting process, and to the moment it is carved and presented, the turkey is the center of attention.

Start with a creamy roasted butternut squash soup. It provides a smooth transition to the main event: Roasted Turkey elegantly dressed with a traditional Cornbread and Sausage Stuffing and Giblet Gravy. With the turkey, stuffing, and gravy as the main attraction, use your time-honored side dishes to round out the meal.

To make a lasting impression, alongside the classic pies you usually make for the dessert course, serve up the Bayou Brandied Pumpkin Pie, Chocolate Pecan Pie, and a mug of warm, Mulled Cider.

# silky sovereign squash soup

YIELD: 12 SERVINGS

2¹/₂ POUNDS (1.1 KG)
  BUTTERNUT SQUASH,
  PEELED AND DICED

6 TABLESPOONS
  VEGETABLE OIL

2¹/₄ CUPS CHOPPED ONION

4 CUPS CHOPPED LEEKS,
  WHITE AND LIGHT GREEN
  PARTS ONLY

1 CUP CHOPPED CARROT

1¹/₂ CUPS CHOPPED CELERY

1 TEASPOON GROUND GINGER

¹/₄ TEASPOON GROUND ALLSPICE

¹/₂ TEASPOON FRESHLY
  GRATED NUTMEG

¹/₂ TEASPOON GROUND CUMIN

1 TEASPOON SALT

³/₄ CUP (175 ML) DRY
  WHITE WINE

3 CUPS (750 ML) APPLE CIDER,
  PLUS EXTRA AS NEEDED

2 QUARTS (2 L) CHICKEN STOCK,
  PLUS EXTRA AS NEEDED

1 BOUQUET GARNI (1 BAY LEAF,
  2 SPRIGS THYME, 5 PARSLEY
  STEMS, 4 STAR ANISE,
  AND 10 BLACK PEPPERCORNS
  BUNDLED IN A PIECE OF
  CHEESECLOTH AND TIED
  WITH STRING)

SALT AND FRESHLY GROUND
  BLACK PEPPER TO TASTE

**1.** Preheat the oven to 425°F (220°C). In a medium roasting pan, toss the squash with 1 tablespoon oil. Cover the pan with aluminum foil and roast for 5 minutes, until softened. Transfer the squash and any juices to a food processor and purée until smooth. Set aside.

**2.** In a large soup pot, heat the remaining 5 tablespoons oil over medium-high heat. Add the onion, leeks, carrot, celery, ginger, allspice, nutmeg, cumin, and salt. Cook, stirring, until the vegetables soften.

**3.** Add the wine and cider and scrape up any browned bits from the bottom of the pot, stirring to dissolve them. Add the reserved squash purée, chicken stock, and bouquet garni. Bring to a boil. Reduce the heat to low and simmer, stirring occasionally, until the vegetables are very tender, about 30 minutes.

**4.** Discard the bouquet garni. Transfer the soup in batches to a food processor and purée until smooth. Strain through a fine sieve into a clean soup pot. Return to the stove and bring to a simmer. Adjust the consistency with additional cider or stock. Season with salt and pepper and serve immediately.

# cranberry relish

1¹/₂ POUNDS (680 G) FRESH
   OR FROZEN CRANBERRIES

1¹/₂ CUPS (340 G)
   GRANULATED SUGAR

PINCH GROUND CINNAMON

1 MEDIUM ORANGE,
   WELL WASHED

1 CUP ORANGE MARMALADE

¹/₂ CUP APPLESAUCE

2 TABLESPOONS FRESH
   LEMON JUICE

**1.** In a heavy, nonreactive saucepan, combine the cranberries, sugar and cinnamon. With a paring knife, carefully remove the peel from the orange, leaving behind the bitter white pith. Finely slice the peel into thin strips and add it to the cranberries. Remove the pith from the orange and discard it, reserving the orange.

**2.** Bring the cranberries to a boil over medium heat. Reduce the heat and simmer. Add the orange marmalade, stirring until the cranberries are cooked and the sugar has dissolved, about 8 to 10 minutes. Remove from the heat and let cool slightly.

**3.** Segment the reserved orange, discard the membranes and any seeds, and place it in a food processor. Chop until pulpy. Stir the orange into the cranberries along with the applesauce and lemon juice.

**4.** Transfer the cranberry sauce to a container and refrigerate overnight before serving.

THANKSGIVING

# radiance roasted turkey
## with cornbread sausage stuffing and giblet gravy

YIELD: 12 SERVINGS

## Turkey

1 9-POUND (4-KG) FRESH TURKEY, GIBLETS, NECK, AND WING TIPS RESERVED

2 TABLESPOONS CHOPPED FRESH SAGE OR 1 TABLESPOON DRIED SAGE

2 TABLESPOONS CHOPPED FRESH THYME OR 1 TABLESPOON DRIED THYME

2 TABLESPOONS CHOPPED FRESH ROSEMARY OR 1 TABLESPOON DRIED ROSEMARY

SALT AND FRESHLY GROUND BLACK PEPPER TO TASTE

2 GRANNY SMITH APPLES, CORED AND CHOPPED

2 YELLOW ONIONS, CHOPPED

2 LARGE ORANGES, PEELED, SECTIONED, AND CHOPPED

1 STALK CELERY, CHOPPED

1. Preheat the oven to 350°F (180°C). Rinse the turkey inside and out with cold water and pat dry with paper towels. In a small bowl, combine the sage, thyme, rosemary, salt, and pepper. Season the turkey inside and out with the herb mixture.

2. In a medium bowl, combine the remaining ingredients. Spoon the apple mixture into the cavity of the turkey and truss the bird with twine. Transfer to a large flameproof roasting pan and roast, uncovered, for 3 hours, or until an instant-read thermometer inserted into the thickest part of the thigh registers 180°F (90°C). The juices that drain from the leg joints should run clear.

3. Transfer to a warmed serving platter and tent with aluminum foil to keep warm. Let rest for 30 minutes. Reserve the roasting pan and its juices.

## Cornbread and Sausage Stuffing

1 POUND (454 G) SWEET ITALIAN SAUSAGE, CASINGS REMOVED

2 CUPS FINELY DICED YELLOW ONION

2 CUPS FINELY DICED CELERY

1 TABLESPOON CHOPPED FRESH SAGE

1 TABLESPOON CHOPPED FRESH ROSEMARY

2 TABLESPOONS CHOPPED FRESH THYME

6 CUPS CORNBREAD CRUMBS

$1^1/2$ CUPS CANNED OR ROASTED (AND PEELED) CHESTNUTS

1 CUP FINELY DICED GRANNY SMITH APPLE

1 CUP CHOPPED FRESH PARSLEY

SALT AND FRESHLY GROUND BLACK PEPPER TO TASTE

1 CUP RAISINS, SOAKED FOR 2 HOURS OR OVERNIGHT IN $1/2$ CUP (125 ML) PORT WINE AND $1/4$ CUP (60 ML) B&B LIQUEUR OR BRANDY

2 CUPS (500 ML) CHICKEN STOCK

1. Preheat the oven to 350°F (180°C). Lightly coat a baking dish with butter or vegetable oil.

2. In a large sauté pan, brown the sausage over medium-high heat. Drain off any excess fat. Add the onion and cook, stirring, until softened and translucent, about 2 minutes. Add the celery and cook for 2 to 3 minutes. Stir in the sage, rosemary, and thyme and transfer to a large bowl.

3. Add the remaining ingredients and stir until well combined. Pour into the prepared baking dish and cover with aluminum foil. Bake for 45 minutes. Remove the foil and bake for 15 minutes more, or until the top is golden brown.

## Giblet Gravy

RESERVED TURKEY GIBLETS, NECK, AND WING TIPS

1 SMALL ONION, SLICED

1/2 CLOVE GARLIC

1 SMALL BAY LEAF

1/8 TEASPOON DRIED BASIL, CRUMBLED

1/8 TEASPOON DRIED ROSEMARY, CRUMBLED

1/8 TEASPOON DRIED THYME, CRUMBLED

SALT AND FRESHLY GROUND BLACK PEPPER TO TASTE

1/4 CUP (30 G) ALL-PURPOSE FLOUR

1. While the turkey is roasting, combine the giblets, neck, wing tips, and 3 cups (750 ml) water in a large saucepan. Add the onion, garlic, bay leaf, herbs, and 1/8 teaspoon salt. Bring to a boil over high heat. Reduce the heat to low and simmer, stirring occasionally, for 15 minutes, or until the liver is tender. Remove the liver and reserve.

2. Continue to simmer the mixture for 1 hour, or until the giblets are tender. Strain, reserving both solids and liquid. Discard the neck, wing tips, vegetables, and bay leaf and chop the giblets and reserved liver. Set aside.

3. When the turkey is done, pour the roasting pan juices into a large glass measuring cup. After the juices separate, measure 1/4 cup (60 ml) fat from the top and return it to the roasting pan. Spoon off and discard any remaining fat in the measuring cup, leaving the turkey juices behind.

4. Sprinkle the flour over the fat in the roasting pan and place over low heat. Cook, stirring, for 2 to 3 minutes. Add 1 cup (250 ml) water, 2 cups (500 ml) reserved giblet stock, and the degreased juices from the measuring cup. Scrape up any browned bits from the bottom of the pan and cook, stirring constantly, until the gravy thickens and bubbles.

5. Strain the gravy into a saucepan. Add the giblets and liver and bring to a boil over high heat. Reduce the heat and simmer, stirring, until the gravy lightly coats a spoon. Serve.

## TIPS FOR A PERFECT BIRD

Allow about 1 pound (450 g) uncooked per person, plus more for leftovers. Larger "toms" have a higher proportion of breast meat than hens.

Try to purchase a natural, free-range turkey for the best flavor. If possible, place an order up to two weeks ahead of time. If you opt for a frozen turkey, remember that you will need to allow time for it to fully thaw.

Stuff the cavity loosely—don't pack it in—so the stuffing reaches the proper internal temperature. Bake extra stuffing in a covered casserole.

Set the turkey on a rack in a large roasting pan to allow maximum air circulation. This will ensure even cooking.

Keep breast meat moist by covering the turkey with aluminum foil for the first 3 to 4 hours of roasting. Then you should remove the foil to brown the skin and baste the breast with cooking juices every half hour.

Add diced aromatic vegetables, such as carrots, celery, and onions, to the roasting pan after uncovering the bird for extra-flavorful turkey and gravy.

Let the turkey rest for 10 minutes before carving.

# baked thanksgiving vegetables

2 SWEET POTATOES, PEELED
AND CUT INTO $1/2$-INCH-THICK
(1.25-CM) SLICES

1 RUSSET POTATO, PEELED
AND CUT INTO $1/2$-INCH-THICK
(1.25-CM) SLICES

3 CARROTS, PEELED AND
CUT INTO $1/2$-INCH-THICK
(1.25-CM) SLICES

1 YELLOW ONION, CUT INTO
$1/2$-INCH-THICK (1.25-CM)
RINGS

1 ACORN SQUASH, PEELED,
HALVED, AND SEEDED; CUT
EACH HALF INTO THIRDS

$1/2$ CUP (100G) PACKED LIGHT
BROWN SUGAR

$1/4$ CUP (60 ML) MAPLE SYRUP

1 TEASPOON PURE VANILLA
EXTRACT

1 TEASPOON GROUND
CINNAMON

4 TABLESPOONS UNSALTED
BUTTER OR MARGARINE,
CUT INTO 8 PIECES

$1/4$ CUP (60 ML) WATER

1. Preheat the oven to 425°F/220°C. In a large bowl, combine the sweet and russet potatoes, carrots, onion, and squash. Add the brown sugar, maple syrup, vanilla, and cinnamon. Toss to coat well.

2. Transfer the vegetables to a rectangular glass baking dish. Dot butter on top of the vegetables and pour the water into the dish. Tightly cover with aluminum foil and bake for 45 minutes.

3. Remove the foil from the baking dish and stir the vegetables. Return the dish to the oven, uncovered, and bake for 15 minutes longer, or until the vegetables are tender and lightly browned. Serve immediately.

## FUN FACT!

During the seven-night *Vision of the Seas* Thanksgiving cruise to the Mexican Riviera, the ship's twenty-four hundred passengers consume approximately 3,000 pounds of fresh vegetables along with 760 pounds of turkey and 13,000 eggs.

THANKSGIVING

# monarch mulled cider
## with winter spices

YIELD: 8 SERVINGS

12 CUPS (3/4 GALLON / 3 L) APPLE CIDER

1/4 CUP (60 ML) FRESH ORANGE JUICE

ZEST (ORANGE PART ONLY) OF 1 ORANGE, CUT INTO STRIPS

1 BAY LEAF

1 TABLESPOON PACKED LIGHT BROWN SUGAR

2 CINNAMON STICKS

2 WHOLE CLOVES

2 WHOLE ALLSPICE

2 TABLESPOONS FRESH LEMON JUICE

PINCH OF SALT

1. In a large saucepan, combine all the ingredients and bring to a boil over high heat. Reduce the heat to medium low and simmer for 30 minutes to blend the flavors.

2. Strain the mulled cider into mugs and serve warm.

# bayou brandied pumpkin pie
## with fruit sauce and créme fraîche

### Pie Shell

1 CUP (110 G) ALL-PURPOSE FLOUR

¹/₂ TEASPOON SALT

¹/₃ CUP (75 G) CHILLED VEGETABLE SHORTENING

5 TO 6 TABLESPOONS ICE WATER

1. In a large bowl, whisk the flour and salt. Using your fingertips, a pastry blender, or 2 knives, work the shortening into the flour until the mixture resembles coarse meal. (Alternatively, combine the ingredients in a food processor, using short pulses.)

2. With a fork, stir in the water, using only as much as needed to gather the mixture into a soft ball of dough. Pat into a disk, cover with plastic wrap, and chill in the refrigerator for at least 1 hour or up to 3 days.

3. Preheat the oven to 450°F (230°C). On a lightly floured surface, roll out the dough into an ¹/₈-inch-thick (3-mm) round. Drape the dough over a rolling pin and fit it into a 10-inch (25-cm) pie pan. Fold the edge under and crimp. Place the pie shell in the freezer for 20 minutes. Remove the shell and prick it all over with the tines of a fork to prevent bubbling during baking.

4. Place a piece of aluminum foil over the dough and fill it with pie weights or dried beans. Place the shell in the oven and bake for 6 minutes. Remove the foil and return to the oven. Bake for an additional 8 to 10 minutes. Place on a wire rack and reserve.

**Note:** Please feel free to use a ready-made pie crust.

### Filling

1 CUP PURÉED PUMPKIN, CANNED

³/₄ CUP (170 G) CRÈME FRAÎCHE (SEE PAGE 136)

¹/₃ CUP (65 G) PACKED DARK BROWN SUGAR

¹/₄ TEASPOON SALT

¹/₂ TEASPOON GROUND CINNAMON

¹/₄ TEASPOON GROUND GINGER

PINCH GROUND CLOVES

2 LARGE EGGS, LIGHTLY BEATEN

1 TEASPOON PURE VANILLA EXTRACT

2 TABLESPOONS BRANDY

1. Preheat the oven to 300°F (150°C). In a large bowl, whisk the pumpkin, crème fraîche, sugar, salt, and spices. Stir in the eggs, vanilla, and brandy until thoroughly combined.

2. Pour the pumpkin filling into the prepared pie shell and jiggle the pan gently to level out the top. Bake for 1 hour, or until lightly set in the center. Transfer to a wire rack and let cool completely. Serve with the fruit sauce (recipe follows).

# fruit sauce

YIELD: 8 SERVINGS

1½ CUPS FRESH RASPBERRIES OR QUARTERED STRAWBERRIES, OR 12 OUNCES (340 G) FROZEN RASPBERRIES OR STRAWBERRIES

5 TABLESPOONS GRANULATED SUGAR OR THE EQUIVALENT IN ARTIFICIAL SWEETENER

1 TABLESPOON FRESH LEMON JUICE, TO TASTE

1. If using fresh fruit: In a blender, combine ½ cup fruit, sweetener, and lemon juice. Blend until smooth. Transfer to a container and stir in the remaining fruit. Chill, covered, until ready to use. If using frozen fruit: Thaw fruit in a sieve over a bowl. In a blender, combine half the drained fruit, the sweetener, and lemon juice. Blend until smooth. Transfer to a container and stir in the remaining drained fruit. Chill, covered, until ready to use. Spoon over each slice of the pie.

Note: You can also serve this sauce with desserts such as cheesecake and pound cake, as well as pancakes.

# crème fraîche

YIELD: 3½ CUPS (875 ML)

2 CUPS (500 ML) HEAVY CREAM

1½ CUPS (375 ML) SOUR CREAM

1. In a small saucepan, heat the heavy cream over low heat, stirring continuously, for approximately 6 minutes, until just lukewarm. Do not boil. Remove from the heat.

2. In a medium mixing bowl, whisk the sour cream until smooth, approximately 2 minutes. Add the lukewarm heavy cream to the sour cream and whisk until well combined. Cover with a clean kitchen towel and let stand at room temperature for 15 hours, or until thick.

3. Transfer the mixture to a container; cover and refrigerate overnight. (The crème fraîche will keep, covered, in the refrigerator for up to 10 days.)

Note: Crème fraîche can be found in the dairy section of gourmet grocery stores.

# chocolate pecan pie

## Pie Crust

1$^1/_2$ CUPS (170 G) ALL-PURPOSE FLOUR,
AND EXTRA FOR DUSTING

1 TEASPOON GRANULATED SUGAR

$^1/_2$ TEASPOON SALT

6 TABLESPOONS UNSALTED BUTTER, CHILLED

3 TABLESPOONS VEGETABLE SHORTENING, CHILLED

4 TABLESPOONS ICE WATER

**1.** In a large bowl, whisk the flour, sugar, and salt. With a knife, cut the butter and shortening into pieces. Using your fingertips, a pastry blender, or 2 knives, work the shortening into the flour until the mixture resembles coarse meal. (Alternatively, combine the ingredients in a food processor, using short pulses.)

**2.** With a fork, stir in the water, using only as much as needed to gather the mixture into a soft ball of dough. Pat into a disk, cover with plastic wrap, and refrigerate for at least 1 hour or up to 3 days.

**3.** Preheat the oven to 400°F/200°C. On a lightly floured surface, roll out the dough into an $^1/_8$-inch-thick (3-mm) round. Drape the dough over a rolling pin and fit it into a 10-inch (25-cm) pie pan. Fold the edge under and crimp. Place the pie shell in the freezer for 20 minutes. Remove the shell and prick it all over with the tines of a fork to prevent bubbling during baking.

**4.** Place a piece of aluminum foil over the dough and fill it with pie weights or beans. Place the shell in the oven and bake for 10 to 12 minutes. Remove the foil and weights and return to the oven. Bake for an additional 8 to 10 minutes. Place on a wire rack and let cool completely.

## Filling

2 CUPS PECAN HALVES

7 OUNCES (200 G) BITTERSWEET
(NOT UNSWEETENED) CHOCOLATE,
CHOPPED INTO $^1/_2$-INCH (1.25-CM) PIECES

3 TABLESPOONS ALL-PURPOSE FLOUR

$^3/_4$ CUP (170 G) UNSALTED BUTTER, SOFTENED

1 CUP (200 G) PACKED DARK BROWN SUGAR

6 LARGE EGGS AT ROOM TEMPERATURE

$^3/_4$ CUP (180 ML) LIGHT CORN SYRUP

$^1/_4$ CUP (60 ML) MOLASSES

1$^1/_2$ TABLESPOONS COINTREAU

2$^1/_4$ TEASPOONS PURE VANILLA EXTRACT

$^1/_2$ TEASPOON SALT

**1.** Reduce the oven to 350°F/180°C. Spread the pecans on a baking sheet and bake for 7 to 10 minutes, until fragrant. Let cool, roughly chop, and place in a medium mixing bowl. Add the chopped chocolate and flour, and stir to mix. Set aside.

**2.** In a large mixing bowl, beat the butter and brown sugar with an electric mixer until light and fluffy. Gradually beat in the eggs, one at a time, stopping 2 or 3 times to scrape down the sides of the bowl. Beat in the remaining ingredients until fully incorporated.

**3.** Add the chocolate mixture to the egg mixture and stir until well combined. Pour the filling into the prepared pie shell and bake for 1 hour, or until lightly set in the center. Transfer to a wire rack and let cool completely before serving.

**Note:** This pie can be kept in the refrigerator, covered in plastic wrap, for up to 1 day. Serve at room temperature and with lightly sweetened whipped cream.

THANKSGIVING

### TIP
# 1

Use a menorah—no matter how ornamental or simple—to create a striking centerpiece. Mini menorahs at each place setting are also a lovely touch.

### TIP
# 2

Assemble small gift packages containing chocolate coins, called *gelt*. Wrap in metallic colors and matching ribbons.

### TIP
# 3

Set out several small clear cruets filled with seasoned olive oil. Guests can dip crusty bread into the oil they put on their plates.

### TIP
# 4

Create the traditional Chanukah color scheme of blue and white with your tablecloth, linen napkins, china, and glassware. Add accents in gold or silver.

### TIP
# 5

Take the time to plan: write a to-do list with the food and decorations to be purchased, and the cleaning and cooking to be done.

### TIP
# 6

Give each place setting two small saucers or bowls for sour cream and applesauce. Use bowls of different colors for a festive look.

### TIP
# 7

Make cookies in the shape of the Star of David or dreidels, and ice the name of each guest on them. Use as place cards.

### TIP
# 8

Fill bowls with nuts, raisins, and *gelt* and set them on the coffee table so you are set to play dreidel after the meal.

# Chanukah

Chanukah, one of the most cherished Jewish holidays, dates back to 165 B.C. and commemorates the rededication of the Temple of Jerusalem. (The word "Chanukah" means "dedicate"). At that time, a small group of Jewish patriots—lead by Judah Maccabee—successfully fought off the Hellenist Syrian invaders who had tried to force the Jewish people to reject their faith.

When the Maccabees reclaimed the Temple of Jerusalem, they cleansed and repaired it but they couldn't find enough undefiled oil to kindle the eternal light, known as the N'er Tamid. In one of the Temple chambers, however, they found a small cruse of oil, but there was only enough to light the lamp for one night. Miraculously, the small amount of oil kept the temple lights burning for eight nights. Almost 2,200 years later, this triumph is still commemorated with the lighting of the menorah.

Chanukah is a very family-centered holiday and the nightly meal is the centerpiece. When it comes to the food itself, there's a lot of latitude. However, must-haves are potato pancakes, or latkes, which are fried and symbolize the miracle of the oil. The rest of the foods served can reflect traditional Jewish cookery. This menu of updated holiday recipes is designed to be flexible—it would make a fantastic Chanukah buffet for the large family gathering, or the individual dishes can be combined in any number of ways to create multiple menus.

# chicken vegetable soup
## with matzo balls

2 LARGE EGGS

1 LARGE EGG WHITE

1/2 TEASPOON SALT

3/4 CUP MATZO MEAL

1 TABLESPOON VEGETABLE OIL

3 TABLESPOONS COLD WATER

8 CUPS (1 L) CHICKEN STOCK

2 MEDIUM PARSNIPS, PEELED
AND CHOPPED

1 LARGE CARROT, PEELED
AND CHOPPED

1 MEDIUM ONION, CHOPPED

1 CUP SLICED WHITE
MUSHROOMS

SALT AND FRESHLY GROUND
BLACK PEPPER TO TASTE

DILL SPRIGS FOR GARNISH

3 TABLESPOONS CHOPPED
FRESH PARSLEY FOR GARNISH

1. In a mixing bowl, whisk the eggs, egg white, and salt. Whisk in the matzo meal, oil, and water. Cover and refrigerate for at least 1 hour or overnight.

2. In a large soup pot, bring the chicken stock to a boil. Add the parsnips, carrot, and onion. Reduce the heat to medium-low and simmer for 5 minutes. Using 2 spoons, gently form the matzo dough into balls 1 to 2 inches (2.5 to 5 cm) in diameter, dropping them into the simmering stock as you make them.

3. Cover the pot and cook the matzo balls, undisturbed, for 15 minutes. Do not lift the lid; the stock must simmer rapidly to allow the matzo balls to expand properly.

4. Uncover the pot and add the mushrooms. Return to a simmer and cook for 2 to 3 minutes. Season with salt and pepper. To serve, ladle the soup into bowls and garnish with the dill and parsley.

# smoked salmon scandinavian
## with onion and capers

1 POUND (450 G) THINLY SLICED
SMOKED SALMON

1 LARGE ONION, THINLY SLICED
INTO RINGS

1/4 CUP CAPERS, DRAINED

8 SPRIGS FRESH PARSLEY

8 LEMON WEDGES

TOAST POINTS

Arrange the salmon slices attractively on 8 plates. Garnish with the onions, capers, parsley sprigs, and lemon wedges. Serve with toast points.

# not-so-traditional beef brisket

1 FIRST-CUT BEEF BRISKET,
4 TO 5 POUNDS (1.8-2.3 KG)

2 TEASPOONS PAPRIKA

SALT AND FRESHLY GROUND
PEPPER TO TASTE

1 MEDIUM CARROT, FINELY
CHOPPED

2 LARGE ONIONS, FINELY
CHOPPED

2 MEDIUM GREEN BELL
PEPPERS, CORED, SEEDED,
AND FINELY CHOPPED

2 TABLESPOONS BRINE-PACKED
GREEN PEPPERCORNS,
DRAINED

10 SMALL NEW POTATOES,
PEELED

4 LARGE CARROTS, CUT INTO
2-INCH (5-CM) PIECES

2 TABLESPOONS GARLIC, MINCED

1. Preheat the oven to 325°F (160°C). Rub the brisket all over with the paprika, salt, and pepper. Scatter the chopped carrot and half the onions and bell peppers over the bottom of a large roasting pan. Top with the brisket. Cover with the remaining onions and bell peppers. Sprinkle with the green peppercorns and season with black pepper.

2. Tuck the new potatoes and carrot pieces around the brisket and cover the pan with 2 heavy layers of aluminum foil, sealing securely. Bake for 4 to 5 hours, or until the meat is very tender.

3. Cut brisket in thin slices and transfer to a large serving platter. Top with the cooked onions, green peppers, and green peppercorns and surround with the potatoes and carrot pieces. Strain the pan juices into a sauceboat and serve alongside.

Note: Serve simply with a rice or noodle dish accompaniment to absorb some of the delicious gravy.

# braised chicken
## with mushrooms and wine

YIELD: 4 SERVINGS

1 TABLESPOON VEGETABLE OIL

2 SPANISH ONIONS, DICED

3 CLOVES GARLIC, MINCED

1½ CUPS WHITE MUSHROOMS, SLICED

½ CUP (125 ML) DRY RED WINE

¼ BUNCH FRESH THYME, CHOPPED

SALT AND FRESHLY GROUND BLACK PEPPER TO TASTE

1 WHOLE CHICKEN, CUT INTO 8 PIECES

1. Preheat the oven to 350°F (180°C).

2. In a large sauté pan, heat the oil over medium-high heat. Add the onions and garlic and cook, stirring, until softened, about 2 minutes. Add the mushrooms and sauté for 5 minutes more.

3. Add the wine and thyme. Cook, stirring, until the liquid is almost evaporated and the mushrooms have absorbed the color and flavor of the wine. Season with salt and pepper.

4. Arrange the chicken pieces in a 9 x 13-inch (23 x 32-cm) baking dish. Pour the mushroom sauce over the chicken and bake for 1¼ hours, or until the chicken is cooked through and the sauce is bubbling.

# potato pancakes
## with spiced apple sauce

### Potato Pancakes

2¼ POUNDS (1 KG) IDAHO POTATOES, PEELED

1 POUND (450 G) ONIONS

2 TABLESPOONS FRESH LEMON JUICE, PLUS EXTRA AS NEEDED

2 LARGE EGGS

¼ CUP (30 G) ALL-PURPOSE FLOUR

¼ CUP MATZO MEAL, PLUS EXTRA AS NEEDED

1 BUNCH CHIVES, CHOPPED

SALT AND FRESHLY GROUND BLACK PEPPER TO TASTE

½ CUP (125 ML) VEGETABLE OIL

1. Preheat the oven to 375°F (190°C). Grate the potatoes and onions into a large nonreactive bowl and toss with the lemon juice to prevent discoloration. Transfer in batches to some cheesecloth or a clean kitchen towel and twist to remove excess moisture. Return to the bowl.

2. Add the eggs, flour, matzo meal and chives. Mix until thoroughly combined. Season with salt and pepper.

3. In a large cast iron skillet or an electric fry pan, heat the oil to 350°F (180°C). (A small piece of bread dropped into the oil should brown within 45 seconds.)

4. Once the oil is hot enough, drop the potato batter into the oil by level serving spoons, being careful not to crowd the pan.

5. Fry the pancakes on one side until lightly browned. With a spatula, carefully turn the pancakes over and fry until browned on the other side.

6. Drain the pancakes on a plate lined with paper towels. Transfer to a baking sheet and bake in the oven until thoroughly browned and crisp, about 8 to 10 minutes. Serve with Spiced Apple Sauce (see accompanying recipe).

### Spiced Apple Sauce

2 POUNDS (900 G) APPLES, PEELED AND SLICED

1 CUP (250 ML) WATER

1 TABLESPOON FRESH LEMON JUICE

¼ CUP (55 G) GRANULATED SUGAR

1 TEASPOON GROUND CINNAMON

1 TEASPOON GROUND ALLSPICE

1. In a large nonreactive Dutch oven, bring the apples, water, and lemon juice to a boil over high heat. Reduce the heat to medium, cover and simmer until the apples are tender, about 20 minutes.

2. Uncover and continue cooking until thickened, about 10 minutes. Remove from the heat.

3. Mash the apples with a potato masher until they become chunky. Stir in the remaining ingredients and transfer to a container. Cover and refrigerate overnight.

# zucchini parmesan potato pancakes

YIELD: 24 PANCAKES

2 POUNDS (900 G) ZUCCHINI

1/2 POUND (225 G) IDAHO
POTATOES, PEELED

1/2 TABLESPOON FRESH
LEMON JUICE

1 CUP CHOPPED SCALLIONS

1/2 CUP GRATED PARMESAN
CHEESE

3/4 CUP CHOPPED FRESH
PARSLEY

1 TABLESPOON PLUS
1 TEASPOON SALT

1/2 TABLESPOON FRESHLY
GROUND BLACK PEPPER

1/3 CUP (40 G) ALL-PURPOSE
FLOUR

1 MEDIUM EGG

VEGETABLE OIL FOR FRYING

1. Preheat the oven to 200°F (95°C) and place a baking sheet in it. Grate the zucchini and potatoes into a large nonreactive bowl and toss with the lemon juice to prevent discoloration. Transfer in batches to cheesecloth or a clean kitchen towel and twist to remove excess moisture. Return to the bowl.

2. Add the scallions, Parmesan, 1/2 cup parsley, 1 tablespoon salt, pepper, flour, and egg. Mix until thoroughly combined.

3. Pour 1/2 inch (1 cm) of oil in the bottom of a large cast iron skillet or an electric fry pan. Heat the oil to 350°F (180°C). (A small piece of bread dropped into the oil should brown within 45 seconds.)

4. Once the oil is hot enough, measure 1/4 cup (60 ml) pancake batter into the pan and flatten it into a small cake with the back of a spoon. Repeat with more batter, being careful not to crowd the pan.

5. Fry the pancakes on one side until the edges start to become crispy and brown, about 5 minutes. With a spatula, carefully turn the pancakes over and fry for about 3 more minutes.

6. Drain the pancakes on a plate lined with paper towels. Transfer to the baking sheet in the oven to keep warm until all the pancakes are made. To serve, place on a platter and sprinkle with the remaining 1/4 cup parsley and 1 teaspoon salt.

# raspberry roll russe

YIELD: 8 SERVINGS

BUTTER AND FLOUR FOR
PREPARING PAN

1½ CUPS (340 G)
GRANULATED SUGAR

6 LARGE EGGS

5 LARGE EGG YOLKS

2 TABLESPOONS CORN SYRUP

2 TABLESPOONS WATER

1 TEASPOON PURE VANILLA
EXTRACT

1¼ CUPS (120 G) CAKE FLOUR

1 TEASPOON BAKING POWDER

½ TEASPOON SALT

⅓ CUP (75 ML) HOT WATER

CONFECTIONERS' SUGAR,
FOR DUSTING

1 CUP RASPBERRY OR
STRAWBERRY JAM

1. Preheat the oven to 450°F (225°C). Lightly coat a 20 x 18-inch (50 x 46-cm) baking sheet with butter and dust with flour. Line with parchment paper and butter and flour the paper. Set aside.

2. In a mixing bowl, combine the sugar, whole eggs, and egg yolks. With an electric mixer, beat on high speed until very foamy, stopping 2 or 3 times to scrape down the sides of the bowl. Gradually beat in the corn syrup, 2 tablespoons water, and vanilla.

3. In a medium bowl, sift together the flour, baking powder, and salt. With a rubber spatula, add the ⅓ cup (75 ml) hot water slowly to the flour mixture, gently folding until just combined.

4. Spread the batter evenly into the prepared baking sheet and bake for 8 minutes, or until the cake springs back when lightly touched.

5. Immediately turn the cake out onto a clean kitchen towel generously dusted with confectioners' sugar. Quickly remove the parchment paper from the bottom of the cake and flip the cake over. While still warm, spread the jam over the cake and then roll it up tightly from the long edge. When cool, place some confectioners' sugar in a sieve and sprinkle it over the roll.

## FUN FACT!

St. Petersburg, Russia, and Tallinn, Estonia, are two of the ports of call on the twelve-night Scandinavia/Russia cruise. St. Petersburg is rich in cultural heritage and is a masterpiece of architecture embodying the soul of Imperial Russia. Estonia was formerly part of the Soviet Union but is now an independent country. In Tallinn, its capital, visitors can walk along the cobblestone streets of the city, one of the oldest on the Baltic Sea. It was founded by the Danes—yes, the Danes!—in the thirteenth century.

## TIP 1

Appetizer ideas: Cheeses with crackers; pre-sliced smoked salmon with dill/mustard sauce and mini rye bread.

## TIP 2

Purchase two tall, thin Christmas topiaries to put on either end of the table and fill the base with a mound of chestnuts.

## TIP 3

For a centerpiece, fill a bowl (sized to nestle into a wreath) with clementines and sprinkle on a few handfuls of cranberries.

## TIP 4

Use plain white dinner plates, and dress up the table with pieces of crystal, china, and silver. Use pieces that can go in the dishwasher to make cleanup easier.

## TIP 5

Create an aroma of Christmas throughout the house: fill a large pot with hot water, add orange rind and cinnamon sticks, and let it simmer on the stove.

## TIP 6

Use as many candlesticks, pillar candles, hurricane lamps, and votives as you can. Keep all candles safely away from fresh greenery.

## TIP 7

Have a collection of Christmas favorites on hand to play as background music, as well as classical music.

## TIP 8

Start the coffee pot before dinner and have the items needed for coffee and tea ready to go. Serve hot cocoa too.

# Christmas

Without a doubt, Christmas Day is the most widely known and celebrated holiday in America. If you love to entertain, the whole Christmas season is not only full of possibilities, but also comes with a kind of excitement and anticipation that exceeds any other holiday.

Christmas in the United States is unlike Christmas anywhere else on the planet. Americans have reinvented the holiday, borrowing snippets of customs from other countries—including decorating trees, sending cards, and giving gifts—to create something distinctly American with freedom to celebrate according to individual family traditions and personal style.

In fact, while we may think that the way we celebrate Christmas in America is centuries old, the truth is that Americans didn't begin to embrace Christmas until the nineteenth century (it was declared a federal holiday in 1870). Thanks to the influence of sentimentalized holiday tales like Charles Dickens's *A Christmas Carol*, the celebration transformed from a raucous holiday resembling the drunken festivities of Mardi Gras—one reason Christmas wasn't celebrated at all in America for two hundred years—into a family-centered day of peace and charity. Americans looked to the great waves of immigrants and cobbled together a new approach to the holiday from the old-country traditions they brought.

Today, we are still evolving how we celebrate. Whether you head up to a mountain cabin, take a cruise on the Caribbean, or stay at home for the holidays, one thing is for sure: food will play a central role in your celebration.

Christmas dinner draws from many traditions—or allows you to create your own from favorite New American recipes. The menu that follows is festive, colorful, and decidedly old-fashioned in concept, but rich, exciting, and graceful, befitting the celebration.

# voyager vegetable beef soup

2 POUNDS (905 G) LEAN STEW
BEEF, CUBED

3¹/₂ QUARTS (3.3 L) WATER

3 MEDIUM ONIONS, CHOPPED

1 TABLESPOON SALT

1¹/₂ TEASPOONS CHOPPED
FRESH THYME

¹/₂ CUP DRIED SPLIT PEAS

1 CUP FRESH OR FROZEN CORN
KERNELS

1 LARGE RUSSET POTATO,
PEELED AND CUBED

1 CUP CHOPPED FRESH SPINACH
LEAVES

1 CUP DICED GREEN BEANS

1 CUP FRESH OR FROZEN PEAS

4 CARROTS, PEELED AND SLICED

1 CUP FRESH OR FROZEN LIMA
BEANS

1 CUP DICED CELERY

1 TABLESPOON TOMATO PASTE

1 MEDIUM GREEN BELL PEPPER,
CORED, SEEDED, AND DICED

2 TABLESPOONS CHOPPED
FRESH PARSLEY

3 MEDIUM TOMATOES, DICED

**1.** In a large soup pot, combine the beef, water, onions, salt, and thyme. Bring to a boil over high heat. Reduce the heat to low and bring to a simmer. Skim the fat and any scum from the surface.

**2.** Add the split peas to the soup, cover, and gently simmer for 90 minutes. Add the remaining ingredients, replace the cover, and simmer for another 30 minutes, until all vegetables are tender. Adjust the seasoning and serve the soup in warmed soup bowls.

**Note:** This is a good soup to cook ahead and reheat when needed.

## FUN FACT!

Christmas is a favorite holiday for many children. That's why Christmas aboard the ships is chock-full of fun, festive activities for them. There's a parade of Santa and his elves and an opportunity to decorate Christmas cookies and take pictures with Santa. In addition, children can view favorite Christmas movies, carol with new-found friends, and partake in many other family activities.

# roasted red pepper salad

## Balsamic Vinaigrette

2 TABLESPOONS
BALSAMIC VINEGAR

1 TABLESPOON FRESH
LEMON JUICE

1/4 TEASPOON DIJON MUSTARD

1/2 CUP (125 ML) EXTRA
VIRGIN OLIVE OIL

SALT AND FRESHLY GROUND
BLACK PEPPER TO TASTE

In a nonreactive bowl, combine the vinegar, lemon juice and mustard. Slowly whisk in the oil. Season with salt and pepper. Cover and refrigerate until ready to use.

## To Assemble

3 BELL PEPPERS IN ASSORTED COLORS

3 RIPE MEDIUM TOMATOES

2 TABLESPOONS PINE NUTS

1/3 CUP GOLDEN RAISINS, SOAKED IN 1/2 CUP (125 ML)
HOT WATER FOR 15 MINUTES AND DRAINED

1 SMALL RED ONION, THINLY SLICED

20 BLACK OLIVES, PITTED AND QUARTERED

3 CLOVES GARLIC, MINCED

1 MEDIUM JALAPEÑO PEPPER, SEEDED AND MINCED

1/8 TEASPOON CAYENNE PEPPER

SALT AND FRESHLY GROUND BLACK PEPPER TO TASTE

1. Place the bell peppers directly over the flame of a gas stove or under the broiler. Roast, turning frequently, until the skin is blackened on all sides. Remove, place in a bowl and cover for 2 minutes. Remove and discard the skin, seeds and core from the bell peppers. Cut the peppers into strips. Place in a nonreactive bowl and reserve.

2. In a medium saucepan, bring 1 quart (1 L) water to a boil. With a paring knife, cut out the stems from the tomatoes and make a small x in the opposite ends. Plunge the tomatoes in the boiling water and leave them in just until the skins are loosened, 10 to 20 seconds. With a slotted spoon, transfer the tomatoes to a bowl of cold water to cool. Slip off the skins and cut the tomatoes in half. Gently but firmly squeeze the seeds from the halves. Dice the tomatoes and add to the peppers.

3. Meanwhile, toast the pine nuts: In a dry skillet over high heat, toss or stir the pine nuts, taking care not to scorch them, until lightly browned. Transfer them to a small bowl, let cool and add to the pepper mixture.

4. Add the remaining ingredients to the pepper mixture. Toss with the balsamic vinaigrette. Cover and refrigerate for at least 2 hours or overnight before serving.

# braised peas

YIELD: 6 SERVINGS

3 TABLESPOONS
  UNSALTED BUTTER

6 GOLDEN SHALLOTS,
  THINLY SLICED

1 CLOVE GARLIC, CRUSHED

1 POUND (454 G) FROZEN PEAS

7/8 CUP (200 ML)
  CHICKEN STOCK

**1.** In a saucepan, heat 2 tablespoons of butter over medium heat. Add the shallots and garlic and cook, stirring, until softened and translucent.

**2.** Add the peas and chicken stock and bring to a boil. Reduce the heat to low and simmer until the peas defrost, about 5 minutes.

**3.** Strain the mixture through a medium sieve over a small saucepan, reserving both liquid and solids. Bring the liquid to a simmer over medium-high heat and reduce to a glaze. Add the reserved peas and toss to coat. Cook until the peas are heated through. Place in a serving dish, top with remaining butter and serve immediately.

**Note:** I prefer using a bag of frozen peas to fresh peas. It is easier and more convenient than having to shell 1 pound (454 g) of peas. Also, sliced mushrooms can be added to this recipe for an added twist. Add them at the same time as the garlic and shallots. Try it, you will like it!

# sweet potato smash
## with chestnuts

YIELD: 6 TO 8 SERVINGS

3 POUNDS (1.4 KG) SWEET
POTATOES, PEELED AND CUT
INTO 1-INCH (3-CM) CHUNKS

1/4 CUP (60 ML) WHOLE MILK

4 TABLESPOONS UNSALTED
BUTTER, SOFTENED

1 CUP WATER-PACKED
CHESTNUTS, DRAINED
AND CHOPPED

SALT AND FRESHLY GROUND
BLACK PEPPER TO TASTE

**1.** In a large saucepan, combine the sweet potatoes with 1/4 inch (1 cm) of water. Bring to a boil over high heat. Reduce the heat to low, cover, and steam for 10 to 12 minutes, or until tender. Drain the potatoes and return them to the saucepan over low heat, to evaporate the small amount of water remaining.

**2.** In a small saucepan, heat the milk and butter over medium-low heat just until the butter melts. Transfer the sweet potatoes to a warmed bowl and mash with a potato masher until smooth. Beat in the warmed milk mixture. Stir in the chestnuts and season with salt and pepper. Serve immediately.

## FUN FACT!

During the seven-night Caribbean Christmas cruise aboard *Rhapsody of the Seas*, the approximately twenty-four hundred guests consume a lot of potatoes—whether they are baked, French fried, or smashed. The total number on the ship's shopping list: 3.25 tons.

# brilliance beef wellington
## with buttery béarnaise

YIELD: 12 SERVINGS

1 TENDERLOIN OF BEEF,
4 POUNDS (1.8 KG)

SALT AND FRESHLY GROUND
BLACK PEPPER TO TASTE

1/2 CUP (125 ML)
VEGETABLE OIL

3 TABLESPOONS UNSALTED
BUTTER

2 1/2 CUPS CHOPPED WHITE
MUSHROOMS

1 MEDIUM ONION, FINELY
CHOPPED

1 CUP (140 G) CHOPPED
FRESH PARSLEY

10 OUNCES (283 G) LIVER PÂTÉ

2 LARGE EGGS

2 POUNDS (1 KG) PREPARED
PUFF PASTRY (AVAILABLE
FROM GOURMET FOOD
STORES)

2 LARGE EGG YOLKS MIXED
WITH 2 TABLESPOONS WATER

**1.** Trim all the fat from the tenderloin. Season with salt and pepper. In a large skillet, heat the oil over medium heat. Add the tenderloin and brown well on all sides. Remove from the pan and let cool.

**2.** Pour off any excess fat from the pan and heat the butter in the same pan over medium heat. Add the mushrooms, onion and parsley. Cook, stirring, until the mushrooms are browned and the onion is translucent. Transfer the contents of the pan to a bowl and let cool.

**3.** Add the liver pâté and eggs to the cooled mushroom mixture and stir until well combined. Cover and refrigerate until ready to use.

**4.** Preheat the oven to 425°F (220°C). Lightly coat a baking sheet with butter. On a lightly floured surface, roll out the puff pastry dough into a 1/4-inch-thick (6-mm) rectangle that is large enough to wrap the tenderloin.

**5.** Spread the pastry with the pâté mixture and place the beef in the center. Wrap the dough tightly around the beef, pressing the edges and ends firmly closed. Lay the bundle seam side down on the prepared baking sheet and brush the top and sides with the egg wash.

**6.** Bake the Wellington for approximately 40 minutes, or until the crust is well browned and the meat is done. (An instant-read thermometer inserted in the center should register 125°F (52°C) for medium-rare or 135°F (57°C) for medium.) Let rest for 10 minutes. Cut into 1- to 1 1/2-inch-thick (2.5-3.75 cm) slices and serve with the Béarnaise sauce (recipe on page 156).

# brilliance buttery béarnaise

YIELD: 2 CUPS

3 STICKS (360 G) UNSALTED BUTTER

2 SHALLOTS, FINELY CHOPPED

6 TABLESPOONS WHITE WINE VINEGAR

2 TABLESPOONS CHOPPED FRESH TARRAGON LEAVES

6 LARGE EGG YOLKS

2 TABLESPOONS FRESH LEMON JUICE

SALT AND FRESHLY GROUND BLACK PEPPER TO TASTE

CAYENNE PEPPER TO TASTE

2 TABLESPOONS CHOPPED FRESH CHERVIL

**1.** Clarify the butter: Melt the butter in a medium saucepan over low heat. Cook until the butterfat becomes clear and the milk solids drop to the bottom of the pan. Skim the surface foam as the butter separates. Carefully spoon the clear butterfat into a second saucepan and keep warm. Discard the milky liquid at the bottom of the first saucepan.

**2.** In a small nonreactive saucepan, combine the shallots, vinegar and tarragon over medium heat. Simmer until the liquid is reduced to 1 tablespoon. Strain and discard the solids.

**3.** Transfer the shallot liquid to the top of a double boiler set over 1 inch (2.5 cm) of simmering (not boiling) water. (If necessary, use a clean kitchen towel to keep the top of the double boiler steady.) Add the egg yolks and lemon juice and season with salt, pepper and cayenne. Gently cook, whisking constantly, until the eggs become foamy. (Do not let the sauce come to a boil.)

**4.** Slowly drizzle in the warm clarified butter, whisking constantly, until the sauce is thickened. Turn off the heat and remove the mixture from the hot water. Strain through a fine sieve into a clean double boiler or a warmed bowl. Adjust the seasonings and stir in the chopped chervil. (Use water to thin the sauce out if necessary.) Keep warm or serve immediately.

## FUN FACT!

Guests aboard action-packed *Brilliance of the Seas* cruises to the British Isles and Norwegian Fjords stop at ten fascinating ports, including Plymouth, England, the seaport from which the Pilgrims set sail in 1620. (England was also home to the British officer for whom Beef Wellington was named.) The cruise also stops in Ireland and Scotland, various destinations in Norway, and the Netherlands.

# holiday ham bake

YIELD: 6 TO 8 SERVINGS

1 3-POUND (1.4-KG) FRESH
BONELESS HAM

4 TABLESPOONS GRANULATED
SUGAR

**1.** With a slicing knife, score the ham: make crosswise slits through the skin and fat $1/2$ inch (1.25 cm) apart, cutting large diamonds. Place the ham in a deep bowl and barely cover with water. Stir in the sugar and cover the bowl with plastic wrap. Let the ham soak in the refrigerator for at least 24 hours.

**2.** Preheat the oven to 200°F/100°C. Line a roasting pan with a piece of aluminum foil that is large enough to wrap up the ham completely. Drain the ham and place it on the foil. Cover the ham with any one of four glazes (see recipes below) and tightly wrap it in the foil.

**3.** Bake the ham for $2^{1}/2$ to 3 hours, unwrapping and basting occasionally with the glaze, until an instant-read thermometer inserted in the center registers 150°F/70°C. After 3 hours remove the ham and increase the oven temperature to 450°F/230°C. Unwrap the ham and baste once again with the glaze. Bake the ham unwrapped for an additional 15 minutes until the skin is crisp.

## ham glazes

For each of the following, combine all the ingredients in a nonreactive bowl.

### Orange Honey Glaze

$1/2$ CUP (125 ML) HONEY

$1/2$ CUP (125 ML) FRESH ORANGE JUICE

JUICE OF 2 LEMONS

2 TABLESPOONS DARK MOLASSES

1 CUP (200 G) LIGHT BROWN SUGAR

### Currant Jelly Glaze

1 CUP CURRANT JELLY

$1/2$ TEASPOON DRY MUSTARD

2 TABLESPOONS PREPARED HORSERADISH

### Cranberry Glaze

1 CUP CRANBERRY JELLY

$1/2$ CUP (125 ML) LIGHT CORN SYRUP

### Mustard Glaze

1 CUP (200 G) LIGHT BROWN SUGAR

$1/4$ CUP (60 ML) PREPARED YELLOW MUSTARD

$1/2$ TEASPOON GROUND CLOVES

# roast ducklings à l'orange

**DUCKS RAISED DOMESTI-CALLY DESCEND FROM ONE OF TWO SPECIES**—the mallard or the muscovy. They can weigh between 3 and 5½ pounds. If you are lucky enough to live in a region where ducks are raised, you can find them fresh from late spring through early winter. Frozen ducks, however, are available year-round almost everywhere.

Fresh ducks should have a broad, fairly plump breast with elastic skin. Frozen ducks should be sealed in packaging that is tight and unbroken. Store fresh duck loosely covered for up to 2 to 3 days in the coldest part of the refrigerator. Thaw frozen duck slowly in the refrigerator; it can take up to 24 to 36 hours to defrost, depending on the size.

**Orange Garnish**

4 ORANGES

**1.** With a vegetable peeler, remove the orange-colored zest (but not the bitter white pith) in pieces from the oranges. Slice half the zest pieces into long julienne strips, reserving the remaining zest pieces for roasting the duck (see Roast Duckling). In a small saucepan, cover the julienne zest with water and bring to a boil. As soon as it boils, strain and return the zest to the saucepan. Repeat the process with more water; drain and reserve.

**2.** With a paring knife, remove all the bitter white pith from the 4 oranges. With a paring knife, carve out the segments from 2 oranges over a bowl to catch any juices; reserve the segments and juice separately. Squeeze the remaining 2 oranges for juice over the same bowl and reserve.

## Roast Duckling

2 4¹/₂-POUND (2-KG)
DUCKLINGS, TRIMMED OF
EXCESS FAT

SALT AND FRESHLY GROUND
BLACK PEPPER TO TASTE

LARGE ZEST PIECES FROM
2 ORANGES
(SEE ORANGE GARNISH)

2 STALKS CELERY, CHOPPED

1 MEDIUM ONION, CHOPPED

2 CUPS (500 ML) VEAL
OR DUCK STOCK

2 TABLESPOONS GRANULATED
SUGAR

1 CUP (250 ML) FRESH ORANGE
JUICE (SEE ORANGE GARNISH)

2 TABLESPOONS WHITE WINE
VINEGAR

¹/₂ TEASPOON CORNSTARCH
(IF NEEDED)

¹/₄ CUP (60 ML) GRAND
MARNIER

JUICE OF 1 LEMON

2 TABLESPOONS UNSALTED
BUTTER

**1.** Preheat the oven to 425°F (220°C). Season the ducks inside and out with salt and pepper. Place the large orange zest pieces in the cavity of each duck and truss the birds with twine. Transfer to a large flameproof roasting pan and roast for 1 to 1¹/₂ hours, basting occasionally with the pan juices. Transfer the ducks to a wire rack over a baking sheet and tent with aluminum foil to keep warm.

**2.** Spoon off all but 2 tablespoons fat from the roasting pan and place the pan over medium heat. Add the celery and onion and cook, stirring, until browned. Add the stock and reduce by half. Reserve.

**3.** In a nonreactive saucepan, combine the sugar and 1 teaspoon water over medium heat. Cook, shaking the pan from time to time, until the mixture caramelizes and turns amber in color. While standing back, carefully add the orange juice, vinegar, reduced stock with its vegetables, and any juices from under the resting ducks. Cook, stirring, until the sauce becomes syrupy, about 10 to 15 minutes.

**4.** Strain the sauce through a fine sieve into a clean saucepan and bring to a simmer over medium heat. With a small ladle, skim the fat from the surface. The sauce should lightly coat the back of a spoon. (If the sauce is too thin, add ¹/₂ teaspoon cornstarch mixed with 2 teaspoons water and cook, stirring, until thickened.) Add the Grand Marnier and lemon juice and stir until combined.

**5.** To serve, cut the ducks in half and divide them among 4 warmed plates. Whisk the butter into the sauce and add the reserved julienne of orange. Pour the sauce over the duck and garnish with the reserved orange segments. Serve immediately.

# christmas yule log

YIELD: 8 TO 10 SERVINGS

1 TABLESPOON VEGETABLE OIL, PLUS EXTRA FOR GREASING

4 LARGE EGGS, SEPARATED

3/4 CUP (170 G) GRANULATED SUGAR, DIVIDED

1 TEASPOON ALMOND EXTRACT

2/3 CUP (65 G) SIFTED CAKE FLOUR

1 TEASPOON BAKING POWDER

1/4 TEASPOON SALT

2 TABLESPOONS CONFECTIONERS' SUGAR

1 RECIPE MOCHA BUTTERCREAM FROSTING

SIFTED COCOA, HOLLY LEAVES, AND/OR CRANBERRIES, FOR GARNISH (OPTIONAL)

**1.** Preheat the oven to 350°F/180°C. Brush the bottom and sides of a 15 x 10-inch (38 x 25-cm) jelly-roll pan with vegetable oil; line it with waxed paper and oil the waxed paper. Dust the pan with a little flour; tilt to coat and tap out the excess. Set aside.

**2.** In a large mixing bowl, beat the egg yolks with an electric mixture at high speed until thick and pale. Slowly add 1/4 cup granulated sugar and beat until well blended. Stir in the oil and almond extract.

**3.** Place the egg whites in a clean, grease-free mixing bowl. With an electric mixer and clean, grease-free beaters, beat on low speed until frothy. Increase the speed to medium and gradually add the remaining 1/2 cup granulated sugar. When the sugar is incorporated, increase the speed to medium-high and beat until the whites hold stiff but not dry peaks. With a rubber spatula, fold the egg whites into the egg yolk mixture until well combined.

**4.** In a small bowl, whisk the flour, baking powder, and salt. With a rubber spatula, gradually fold the dry ingredients into the egg mixture. Spread the batter evenly into the prepared baking sheet.

**5.** Bake the cake for 8 minutes, or until the center springs back when lightly touched.

**6.** While the cake is baking, sift the confectioner's sugar into a 15 x 10-inch (38 x 25-cm) rectangle on a clean kitchen towel. When the cake is done, immediately turn it out onto the towel and quickly remove the waxed paper from the bottom. While still warm, roll the cake and towel together from the shorter end and let cool completely on a wire rack, seam side down.

**7.** When cool, unroll the cake and remove the kitchen towel. Spread 1 cup mocha buttercream frosting over the cake and then re-roll it. Place the roll seam side down on a serving plate and spread with the remaining frosting.

**8.** Refrigerate the Yule log for at least 1 hour before serving. Garnish, if desired, with sifted cocoa, holly leaves, and/or cranberries.

# mocha buttercream frosting

YIELD: 2 CUPS

1/2 CUP (115 G) UNSALTED BUTTER OR MARGARINE, AT ROOM TEMPERATURE

5 CUPS (550 G) SIFTED CONFECTIONERS' SUGAR

1/3 CUP (40 G) UNSWEETENED COCOA POWDER

1/2 (125 ML) CUP STRONG BREWED COFFEE, COLD

2 TEASPOONS PURE VANILLA EXTRACT

In a bowl, beat the butter or margarine with an electric mixer at medium speed until creamy. Beat in the sugar, cocoa, and half the coffee. Beat in the vanilla. Add enough remaining coffee to reach the desired spreading consistency.

# gingerbread house dough

YIELD: 1 GINGERBREAD HOUSE OR 30 COOKIES

2 CUPS (250 G) VEGETABLE SHORTENING (NO SUBSTITUTES)

2 CUPS (250 G) GRANULATED SUGAR

2 CUPS (500 ML) DARK MOLASSES

3 TABLESPOONS GROUND CINNAMON

2 TEASPOONS BAKING SODA

1 TEASPOON SALT

9 CUPS (1 KG) ALL-PURPOSE FLOUR, APPROXIMATELY

**1.** In a large saucepan, combine shortening, sugar, and molasses. Cook, stirring, over low heat until the sugar is dissolved. Remove from the heat and add the cinnamon, baking soda, and salt.

**2.** Stir in the flour, one cup at a time, until the dough can be formed into a ball. Lightly flour a work surface or wooden board. Turn the dough onto the board and knead until even in color and smooth (not crumbly and dry), adding more flour if necessary.

**3.** Form the dough into a log and cut into 5 equal pieces. Wrap the dough pieces in plastic wrap and refrigerate overnight before using for your gingerbread house or gingerbread cookies. When ready to bake, place in a 375°F/190°C oven for 25 minutes.

# apple applause

## baked apples with vanilla syrup and crème anglaise

### Crème Anglaise

1 CUP (225 G) GRANULATED SUGAR

12 LARGE EGG YOLKS

1 QUART (1 L) WHOLE MILK

1 TABLESPOON PURE VANILLA EXTRACT

**1.** Prepare a large bowl of ice water. In a mixing bowl, whisk the sugar and egg yolks until pale in color, about 2 minutes. Set aside.

**2.** Pour the milk into the top of a double-boiler set over 1 inch (2.5 cm) of simmering (not boiling) water. Remove and discard the skin that forms on the top and slowly pour half of the milk into the egg yolk mixture, gently whisking until well blended.

**3.** Return the egg yolk mixture to the double-boiler and place over medium-low heat. Gently cook, stirring continually with a wooden spoon, until the mixture thickens and lightly coats the back of the spoon and an instant-read thermometer registers 185°F/85°C. (The mixture should not be allowed to boil.)

**4.** Immediately remove the mixture from the heat and strain through a fine sieve into a clean bowl. Place the bowl in the larger bowl of ice water to chill the sauce down quickly and prevent curdling. Stir in the vanilla. When cool, cover with plastic wrap and chill in the refrigerator until ready to use.

### Baked Apples

2 CUPS GOLDEN RAISINS

4 DRIED FIGS, FINELY DICED

$2/3$ CUP (55 G) SLIVERED ALMONDS

2 TEASPOONS GRATED ORANGE ZEST

PINCH GROUND CINNAMON

PINCH FRESHLY GRATED NUTMEG

$1/2$ CUP (125 ML) COGNAC OR BRANDY

$1/2$ CUP (125 ML) MUSCAT WINE

12 GRANNY SMITH APPLES, CORED BUT LEFT WHOLE AND UNPEELED

1 CUP (200 G) LIGHTLY PACKED LIGHT BROWN SUGAR

1 STICK (120 G) UNSALTED BUTTER, SOFTENED

$2/3$ CUP (150 G) GRANULATED SUGAR

3 CUPS (750 ML) DRY WHITE WINE

2 VANILLA BEANS, SPLIT

**1.** In a large nonreactive bowl, combine the raisins, figs, almonds, orange zest, cinnamon, nutmeg, cognac or brandy, and Muscat. Cover and refrigerate overnight.

**2.** With a sharp knife, score the skins of the apples along their circumference to prevent them from splitting during cooking. Stuff the apples with the raisin mixture, slightly overfilling them. Mash the brown sugar with the butter and spread the mixture over the tops of the apples.

**3.** Preheat the oven to 300°F (150°C). In a small saucepan, combine the granulated sugar and wine and bring to a boil. Reduce the heat to low and use the tip of a blunt knife to scrape the vanilla bean seeds into the syrup. Gently simmer, stirring occasionally, until the vanilla has infused the syrup, about 5 minutes.

**4.** Remove the vanilla beans from the syrup and pour the syrup into a baking dish. Arrange the stuffed apples in the dish and bake for 1¼ hours, basting occasionally with the syrup, until the apples are tender but not mushy. If the syrup begins to caramelize, add enough water to cover the bottom of the dish. (As the apples cook, the syrup takes on their flavor and forms their sauce.)

**5.** To serve, divide the apples among dessert plates and spoon the syrup over them. Serve with the crème anglaise in a sauceboat on the side.

# grandeur glögg

1¼ CUPS (320 ML) WATER

1 TEASPOON DRIED CARDAMOM
 SEEDS OR 8 WHOLE
 CARDAMOM PODS

5 WHOLE CLOVES

2 CINNAMON STICKS

1 STRIP ORANGE ZEST

¼ CUP RAISINS, PLUS EXTRA
 FOR GARNISH

10 BLANCHED ALMONDS, PLUS
 EXTRA FOR GARNISH

½ CUP (115 G) GRANULATED
 SUGAR

2 BOTTLES RED WINE

1¼ CUPS (320 ML) COGNAC
 OR UNFLAVORED AQUAVIT
 (SEE NOTE)

¾ CUP (175 ML) PORT WINE

**1.** In a large nonreactive saucepan, bring the water, spices, orange zest, raisins, and almonds to a boil. Reduce the heat and simmer for 5 minutes. Remove from the heat and let stand for 30 minutes to allow the flavors to blend.

**2.** Strain the mixture through a sieve into another saucepan and stir in the sugar until dissolved. Stir in the red wine, Cognac or aquavit, and port. Heat over low heat until hot but not boiling.

**3.** To serve, ladle into mugs. Add a few raisins and almonds to each mug and serve immediately.

**Note:** If you do not have Cognac or aquavit (a typical Scandinavian alcohol) you can use whisky instead.

# nordic **eggnog**

YIELD: 4 SERVINGS

5 LARGE EGGS, SEPARATED

3/4 CUP (175 ML) CANNED
SWEETENED CONDENSED MILK

1 TABLESPOON GRANULATED
SUGAR

1 1/4 TEASPOONS PURE
VANILLA EXTRACT

5 1/3 CUPS (1.3 L) WHOLE MILK

2 1/2 TABLESPOONS RUM,
PLUS EXTRA TO TASTE

1/4 TEASPOON FRESHLY
GRATED NUTMEG

**1.** In a large mixing bowl, beat the egg yolks with an electric mixer until thickened and light. Gradually stir in the condensed milk, sugar, vanilla, and milk.

**2.** With clean beaters, beat the egg whites in another large bowl until stiff peaks form. With a spatula, fold the egg whites into the milk mixture.

**3.** Stir the rum into the mixture. Garnish with the nutmeg and serve immediately.

## TIP 1

Create a separate Kwanzaa display on a table not used for dining: a harvest display of winter vegetables and tropical fruits is beautiful.

## TIP 2

Start a Kwanzaa Memory Book and add entries each year. Note the theme, menu, decorations, guests, and what you learned.

## TIP 3

Seat your guests so that the oldest members of the group are next to the youngest.

## TIP 4

Play diverse kinds of music, from contemporary black artists to authentic tribal music from Africa.

## TIP 5

Try to serve the meal family style rather than buffet style since this is a holiday that celebrates community.

## TIP 6

Rustic bowls filled with tropical fruits can make a lovely addition to the room decor, as can hollowed-out gourds filled with almonds.

## TIP 7

Buy red, green, and black candles but use fabric colors in traditional African costumes for the rest of your color scheme.

## TIP 8

Many traditional African stews are made in a *canari*, or terra-cotta pot. You can bring the clay cooker right to the table.

# Kwanzaa

Kwanzaa embodies everything that entertaining should be about: it's a time of celebration, community gathering, cultural awareness, history, thanks-giving, reflection, creativity, self-expression, love, and food.

While many Americans think that Kwanzaa is an entirely new holiday, it is actually rooted in celebrations recorded in African history as far back as ancient Egypt and which continue to this day among certain tribes and regions in Africa. Drawing and expanding on the traditions of "first-fruit" harvest festivals celebrated throughout Africa, Kwanzaa was established in America in 1966 by Dr. Maulana Karenga to bring African Americans together in celebration of their African culture.

Kwanzaa begins on December 26 and is celebrated over seven days. Each day focuses on one of the seven principles of Kwanzaa: Unity, Self-determination, Collective Work and Responsibility, Cooperative Economics, Purpose, Creativity, and Faith. There are also the Seven Symbols of Kwanzaa, which families arrange in a beautiful display to reflect their African heritage: the Mat, the Unity Cup, the Crops, the Candleholder, the Seven Candles, the Corn, and the Gifts.

During each night of Kwanzaa, the family gathers and a child lights one of the seven candles. One of the seven principles is then discussed. On the sixth day, which falls on New Year's Eve, family and friends gather to enjoy a large feast called a Karamu, which celebrates their history and the upcoming new year.

People generally try to create a menu that reflects some aspect of their African heritage—and that covers a lot of territory. Try to incorporate traditional African dishes and fare from countries all over the world inhabited by people of African heritage. The Kwanzaa menu here is simple, symbolic, and delicious.

# crispy chicken cameroon
## with apricot dipping sauce

YIELD: 4 SERVINGS

1 CUP (75 G) SWEETENED
FLAKED COCONUT

1/2 CUP (60 G)
ALL-PURPOSE FLOUR

1/2 TEASPOON SALT

1/4 TEASPOON FRESHLY GROUND
BLACK PEPPER

1/4 TEASPOON GARLIC POWDER

1 1/2 POUNDS (680 G)
BONELESS, SKINLESS
CHICKEN BREAST, CUT INTO
1-INCH (3-CM) STRIPS

1 LARGE EGG, LIGHTLY BEATEN

1/3 CUP (75 G) UNSALTED
BUTTER OR MARGARINE,
MELTED

1 CUP (250 ML) APRICOT
PRESERVES

2 TEASPOONS DIJON MUSTARD

1. Preheat the oven to 400°F (200°C). In a shallow bowl, combine the coconut, flour, salt, pepper, and garlic powder.

2. Dip each chicken strip into the beaten egg, shaking off the excess, then immediately dredge in the coconut mixture. Arrange on a shallow baking pan and drizzle with the melted butter.

3. Bake the chicken strips for 25 minutes, turning once, until the chicken is browned and cooked through. Meanwhile, in a small bowl stir together the apricot preserves and mustard until well blended. Serve the chicken strips with the apricot dipping sauce.

# chilled buttermilk tomato and avocado soup

## Soup

3 POUNDS (1.4 KG) RIPE
TOMATOES

2 TABLESPOONS TOMATO PASTE

1 CUP (250 ML) BUTTERMILK

1 TABLESPOON EXTRA VIRGIN
OLIVE OIL

1 RIPE HAAS AVOCADO

JUICE OF 1 LEMON

1 TABLESPOON FINELY
MINCED FRESH PARSLEY

SALT AND FRESHLY GROUND
BLACK PEPPER TO TASTE

HOT PEPPER SAUCE, SUCH
AS TABASCO, TO TASTE

1. In a large saucepan, bring 2 quarts (2 L) water to a boil. Meanwhile, with a paring knife, cut out the stems from the tomatoes and make a small X in the opposite ends. Working in batches, plunge the tomatoes in the boiling water and leave them in just until the skins are loosened, 10 to 20 seconds. With a slotted spoon, transfer the tomatoes to a large bowl of cold water to cool. Slip off the skins and cut the tomatoes in half. Gently but firmly squeeze the seeds from the halves.

2. Transfer the tomatoes to a food processor or food mill. Process or grind the tomatoes until smooth. Press the tomato purée through a sieve into a large nonreactive bowl. Stir in the tomato paste, buttermilk, and oil.

3. Peel and pit the avocado and press it through the sieve into a small bowl. Stir 1 tablespoon lemon juice into the avocado and then add the avocado mixture, remaining lemon juice, and parsley to the tomato mixture. Stir well and season with salt, pepper, and hot pepper sauce. Transfer to a container and refrigerate for several hours.

### To Assemble

1 CUCUMBER, PEELED, SEEDED, AND DICED

1 CUP (250 ML) SOUR CREAM OR PLAIN YOGURT

Adjust the seasonings in the chilled soup if necessary and ladle it into chilled soup bowls. Pass the cucumber, sour cream, and extra hot pepper sauce separately.

# bahamas bake
## chicken curry

¼ CUP (30 G) PLUS
  1 TABLESPOON
  ALL-PURPOSE FLOUR

1½ TEASPOONS SALT

¾ TEASPOON FRESHLY GROUND
  BLACK PEPPER

2½ POUNDS (1.1 KG)
  CHICKEN PIECES
  (THIGHS, DRUMSTICKS,
  AND BREASTS)

2 TABLESPOONS UNSALTED
  BUTTER OR MARGARINE

1 CUP COARSELY CHOPPED
  PEELED APPLE

½ CUP CHOPPED ONION

1 CUP (75 G) PLUS
  2 TABLESPOONS SWEETENED
  FLAKED COCONUT

1 CLOVE GARLIC, MINCED

3 TEASPOONS CURRY POWDER

1½ (375 ML) CUPS
  CHICKEN STOCK

1. Preheat the oven to 400°F (200°C). In a medium bowl, combine ¼ cup (30 g) flour, the salt, and pepper. Dredge the chicken pieces in the flour mixture and shake off the excess. Arrange the chicken skin-side up in a single layer in a shallow baking pan. Dot with 1 tablespoon butter. Bake the chicken for 15 to 20 minutes, or until it begins to brown.

2. Meanwhile, in a medium saucepan, heat the remaining 1 tablespoon butter over medium-high heat. Add the apple, onion, 2 tablespoons coconut, garlic, and curry powder. Cook, stirring, until the onion is softened but not browned. Stir in the remaining 1 tablespoon flour and chicken stock. Bring to a boil and remove from the heat.

3. Reduce the oven temperature to 350°F (180°C). Pour the curry sauce over the chicken in the baking pan and sprinkle with the remaining 1 cup coconut. Bake for 20 to 25 minutes, or until the chicken is cooked through. Transfer the chicken and sauce to a warmed serving platter and serve with hot rice, if desired.

# baked plantains

½ CUP (115 G) UNSALTED
  BUTTER, MELTED

⅔ CUP (135 G) BROWN SUGAR

PINCH GROUND CINNAMON

PINCH GRATED NUTMEG

6 LARGE RIPE PLANTAINS,
  LEFT IN THEIR SKINS AND
  WELL WASHED

1. Preheat the oven to 375°F (190°C). In a small bowl whisk the melted butter, sugar, cinnamon, and nutmeg until well combined.

2. Slice each plantain in half lengthwise starting through the skin of its inner edge but leaving the outer edge intact. Pry open each plantain a bit and arrange them cut side up in a baking dish. Brush the sugar mixture over the plantains in their skins and bake for approximately 25 minutes, or until they are soft. Serve immediately.

# african vegetable stew

YIELD: 4 SERVINGS

1 BUNCH SWISS CHARD

2 TABLESPOONS CANOLA OIL

1 VERY LARGE ONION, CHOPPED

1 CLOVE GARLIC, CHOPPED

2 MEDIUM YAMS, SCRUBBED
WELL OR PEELED

1 15-OUNCE (425 G) CAN
CHICKPEAS OR GARBANZO
BEANS, DRAINED

1/2 CUP RAISINS

1/2 CUP RAW RICE

5 MEDIUM TOMATOES,
CHOPPED, OR 1 28-OUNCE
(800 G) CAN PEELED
TOMATOES WITH THEIR JUICE

SALT AND FRESHLY GROUND
BLACK PEPPER TO TASTE

HOT PEPPER SAUCE, SUCH
AS TABASCO, TO TASTE

1. Rinse the chard in several changes of cold water and drain. Strip off the leaves, reserving them separately from the white stems. Chop the leaves coarsely and slice the stems crosswise into 1/4-inch (.5-cm) slices.

2. In a large skillet, heat the oil over medium heat. Add the onion, garlic, and chard stems and cook, stirring, until the vegetables are barely limp. Add the chopped chard leaves and cook, stirring, until just wilted.

3. Slice the yams into 1/4-inch (.5-cm) slices and add them to the skillet along with the chickpeas, raisins, rice, and tomatoes. Season with salt, pepper, and hot pepper sauce. Cook, stirring gently, until the rice and yams are tender, approximately 20 minutes. Serve immediately.

# benne cakes

YIELD: 1 DOZEN

1 CUP (200 G) TIGHTLY PACKED LIGHT BROWN SUGAR

1/4 CUP (55 G) UNSALTED MARGARINE, SOFTENED

1 LARGE EGG, BEATEN

1/2 TEASPOON PURE VANILLA EXTRACT

1 TEASPOON FRESH LEMON JUICE

1/2 TEASPOON BAKING POWDER

1/2 CUP (110 G) ALL-PURPOSE FLOUR

1/4 TEASPOON SALT

1 CUP SESAME SEEDS, TOASTED

1. Preheat the oven to 230°F (160°C). Lightly oil a baking sheet.

2. In a large bowl, combine the brown sugar and butter. With an electric mixer, beat until creamy. Add the egg, vanilla, and lemon juice and stir until combined. Stir in the flour, baking powder, salt, and sesame seeds.

3. Drop rounded teaspoons of the dough 2 inches (5 cm) apart onto the prepared baking sheet. Bake for 15 minutes, or until the edges are dark golden. Transfer to a wire rack to cool.

Note: "Benne," or sesame seeds, are eaten for good luck.

## FUN FACT!

Although Royal Caribbean International doesn't have ports of call in Africa, a safari experience is only a solarium away. Guests aboard *Radiance of the Seas* can enjoy an indoor/outdoor pool area with three sixteen-foot-high stone elephants and cascading waterfalls surrounded by live jungle-like vegetation.

## TIP 1

Let your child choose the colors and theme for the party decorations. Party supply stores put together wonderful birthday kits.

## TIP 2

Buy disposable cameras for guests (if they're old enough) and let them snap away. They can take the cameras home with them.

## TIP 3

Invite the parents of your child's friends to attend. It's a time to get to know them better and it's also a way of thanking them for carpools and play dates.

## TIP 4

Include healthy, fun snacks. Give each child a colorful plastic cup with his or her name on it. Fill halfway with popcorn, then poke in carrot, celery, and bread sticks.

## TIP 5

Photocopy photographs of the birthday boy or girl. Enlarge them until they're the size of the sheet of paper. Hang these around the party area.

## TIP 6

When parents call to RSVP be sure to ask if their children have any food allergies so you can prepare special foods.

## TIP 7

Remove any fragile objects from the party area. You may also want to roll up smaller rugs and store them until the party is over.

## TIP 8

Make writing thank you notes a fun activity by supplying your child with stickers and gel pens in bright colors.

# Child's Birthday Party

Birthdays are joyous occasions to plan for and celebrate with as much enthusiasm as any of the "big" holidays. Each year, I make my children's birthday parties as special as possible—it's a wonderful gift I can give them.

After all, birthdays are not a trivial matter. Thousands of years ago, birthdays were important because humans linked their ultimate fate with the movements of the stars—knowing your birth date and following its astrological advice was considered imperative to having a happy life.

Many modern-day birthday traditions in America originally hailed from Germany, where it was customary for birthday boys or girls to receive gifts, to be permitted to choose their own menus, and to be celebrated with candle-ringed butter cakes. The tradition of candles on the cake, however, is as old as the ancient worshipers of the Greek moon goddess Artemis, who was honored with moon-shaped honey cakes surrounded by lit tapers.

I love the idea of letting children choose their own menus. The recipes here reflect the kinds of foods they will instinctively desire: hot dogs, pizza, chicken nuggets, pigs in a blanket, and spaghetti.

Over the years, I've discovered that the best way to handle beverages during a children's party is to make a big bowl of punch. My Lively Lemony Lemonade has received rave reviews from the most candid food critics of all time—my children's friends.

The major moment of the day is the presentation of the cake and the singing of "Happy Birthday!" I've included a crowd-pleasing Strawberry Celebration Cake, but because the cake is of such importance to the guest of honor, allow your child to have the final say on the cake's flavor, icing, color, and shape.

# adventure-ous sandwich surprise

YIELD: 4 SERVINGS

8 SLICES GOOD-QUALITY
WHITE BREAD

1 CUP PEANUT BUTTER, SMOOTH
OR CHUNKY

2 LARGE RIPE BANANAS, PEELED
AND SLICED

4 TABLESPOONS STRAWBERRY
PRESERVES

Spread each slice of bread with some peanut butter. Arrange the banana slices in an even layer on 4 bread slices. Spoon 1 tablespoon preserves on each banana-topped bread slice. Top with the other slice of bread and cut diagonally.

# florida fruit fiesta

YIELD: 4 SERVINGS

1/2 CUP PEELED AND
DICED APPLE

1/2 CUP PEELED AND
DICED BANANA

1/2 CUP PEELED AND
DICED CANTALOUPE

1/2 CUP PEELED AND DICED
HONEYDEW MELON

1/2 CUP SEEDLESS GRAPES,
GENTLY WASHED

1/2 CUP STRAWBERRIES,
GENTLY WASHED, TRIMMED,
AND QUARTERED

1/2 PINEAPPLE, PEELED
AND DICED

1/2 CUP PEELED, SECTIONED,
AND DICED ORANGE

1 TABLESPOON UNSWEETENED
FLAKED COCONUT

1 CUP WHIPPED TOPPING

In a chilled nonreactive mixing bowl, combine all the fruit. Just before serving, add the coconut and whipped topping and stir to combine.

Note: You may substitute other fruits, such as watermelon, kiwi, blackberries, raspberries, blueberries, or peaches.

## FUN FACT!

The approximately 212,000 children between the ages of 3 and 17 who cruise each year aboard Royal Caribbean ships can participate in lots of fun activities. This is especially true on the new Voyager-class ships, which include ice skating rinks, rock climbing walls, and in-line tracks for skateboarding. In addition, the Adventure Ocean Youth program provides activities specially tailored to children in different age groups.

# spaghetti sicily

2 TABLESPOONS PURE
  OLIVE OIL

1 CUP CHOPPED ONION

3 8-OUNCE (226 G) CANS
  TOMATOES, DRAINED AND
  CHOPPED

1 6-OUNCE (170 G) CAN
  TOMATO PASTE

1 TEASPOON DRIED BASIL

1 TEASPOON DRIED OREGANO

1 TABLESPOON GRANULATED
  SUGAR

SALT AND FRESHLY GROUND
  BLACK PEPPER TO TASTE

2 POUNDS (900 G) DRIED
  SPAGHETTI OR ANY OTHER
  TYPE OF PASTA

1. In a large skillet, heat the oil over medium heat. Add the onion and cook, stirring, until softened and translucent, about 8 minutes.

2. Add the tomatoes and tomato paste and stir until well combined. Stir in the basil, oregano, and sugar. Season with salt and pepper. Bring to a simmer and cook, stirring occasionally, until thickened, about 1 hour. Adjust the seasonings.

3. Cook the spaghetti in a stockpot of boiling salted water until *al dente*, 6 to 8 minutes. Drain the pasta and return it to the pot. Add two-thirds of the sauce and toss to coat. To serve, transfer the pasta to a large, warmed serving bowl and top with the remaining sauce. Serve immediately.

# chicken littles

NONSTICK COOKING SPRAY

3 BONELESS, SKINLESS
CHICKEN BREAST HALVES

1 LARGE EGG WHITE,
LIGHTLY BEATEN

1/2 CUP CRUSHED CORNFLAKES

1 TEASPOON GARLIC SALT

1 TEASPOON PAPRIKA

1/4 TEASPOON FRESHLY GROUND
BLACK PEPPER

1/2 CUP GRATED
PARMESAN CHEESE

KETCHUP

1. Preheat the oven to 375°F (190°C). Lightly coat a nonstick baking sheet with cooking spray.

2. Rinse the chicken breasts well under cold running water and blot dry with paper towels. Cut each breast into 1-inch-thick (2.5-cm) slices.

3. In a small bowl, beat the egg white until stiff peaks form. In a shallow dish, combine the cornflakes, garlic salt, paprika, black pepper, and Parmesan.

4. Quickly dip the chicken pieces in the egg white and then roll in the cornflake mixture. Transfer to the prepared baking sheet.

5. Bake the chicken pieces for 20 minutes, or until cooked through and crispy but not dry. Let cool slightly before serving with ketchup on the side.

# pillowy pigs

NONSTICK COOKING SPRAY

1 12-OUNCE (340 G) CAN
REFRIGERATED BISCUIT DOUGH

4 ALL-BEEF HOT DOGS

KETCHUP AND MUSTARD

1. Preheat the oven to 350°F (180°C). Lightly coat a nonstick baking sheet with nonstick cooking spray.

2. Wrap 2 biscuits around each hot dog, pinching the dough to seal the "blanket." Transfer the bundles to the prepared baking sheet, leaving plenty of room between them for expansion.

3. Bake for 10 minutes, or until the dough is golden brown. Serve with ketchup and mustard on the side.

# mama mia mac and cheese
## with parmesan crumb topping

YIELD: 6 TO 8 SERVINGS

**Parmesan
Crumb Topping**

4 TABLESPOONS
   UNSALTED BUTTER

2$^1$/$_2$ CUPS DRIED BREAD CRUMBS

$^3$/$_4$ CUP GRATED
   PARMESAN CHEESE

2 TABLESPOONS CHOPPED
   FRESH PARSLEY

In a sauté pan, melt the
butter over medium heat.
Add the bread crumbs and
toss to coat. Stir in the
Parmesan cheese and parsley
and transfer to a bowl.
Cover and refrigerate until
ready to use.

**Macaroni and Cheese**

1 POUND (450 G) ELBOW MACARONI

4 TABLESPOONS UNSALTED BUTTER

1 CLOVE GARLIC, MINCED

2 TABLESPOONS ALL-PURPOSE FLOUR

3 CUPS (750 G) WHOLE MILK

$^1$/$_2$ CUP (125 ML) HEAVY CREAM

4 CUPS GRATED SHARP CHEDDAR CHEESE

1 TEASPOON SALT, PLUS EXTRA AS NEEDED

$^1$/$_2$ TEASPOON FRESHLY GROUND BLACK PEPPER, PLUS EXTRA AS NEEDED

$^1$/$_2$ TEASPOON DRY MUSTARD

1. Preheat the oven to 375°F (190°C). Lightly coat a 13 x 9-inch
(32 x 23-cm) ovenproof baking dish or casserole with butter.
Cook the macaroni in a stockpot of boiling salted water until
*al dente*, 6 to 8 minutes. Drain, transfer to a large bowl, and toss
with 1 tablespoon butter. Set aside.

2. In a large saucepan, melt the remaining 3 tablespoons butter
over medium-low heat. Add the garlic and cook, stirring, for
1 minute. Whisk in the flour and cook, stirring, until the mixture
begins to bubble (do not let the mixture darken in color).

3. Remove the mixture from the heat and gradually whisk in the
milk, stirring to dissolve any lumps. Return to the heat and bring
to a simmer. Cook, stirring constantly, until thickened.

4. Reduce the heat to low and gradually stir in the cream,
cheese, 1 teaspoon salt, $^1$/$_2$ teaspoon pepper, and mustard. Adjust
the seasonings. Stir the sauce into the macaroni and
transfer the mixture to the prepared baking dish. (The unbaked
macaroni and cheese will keep, covered, in the refrigerator
for up to 2 days.)

5. Sprinkle the Parmesan crumb topping evenly over the
macaroni and cheese and bake for 30 minutes, or until golden
brown and bubbling.

# pizza minis

2 TABLESPOONS PURE
OLIVE OIL

1 LARGE CLOVE GARLIC, MINCED

8 MINI BAGELS, SLICED IN HALF

2 CUPS GRATED
MOZZARELLA CHEESE

1 CUP (250 ML) PREPARED
TOMATO SAUCE

2 TO 3 TEASPOONS MIXED
DRIED HERBS (BASIL,
PARSLEY, AND OREGANO)

1. Preheat the oven to 450°F (230°C). In a small bowl, combine the oil and garlic. Brush half the oil mixture on the bagel halves. Cover the bagel halves with half the cheese.

2. Spoon about 1 tablespoon tomato sauce onto each bagel half. Top with the remaining cheese and herbs. Drizzle with the remaining oil mixture.

3. Transfer the mini pizzas to a baking sheet and bake for 8 to 10 minutes, or just until the bread starts to get crisp. Serve immediately.

Note: Additional toppings such as fresh vegetables or pepperoni may be added.

# grandeur grilled cheese

4 TABLESPOONS UNSALTED
BUTTER

8 SLICES GOOD-QUALITY
WHITE BREAD

8 SLICES AMERICAN CHEESE

2 RIPE TOMATOES, CUT INTO
4 SLICES EACH

1. In a sauté pan, melt 1 tablespoon butter, swirling it around in the pan. Add 2 bread slices side by side. Top each with 1 slice cheese. Cook the bread slices until the undersides begin to brown, about 5 minutes.

2. Top each cheese-topped slice of bread with 2 slices tomato, another slice of cheese, and a slice of bread. With a spatula, flip the sandwich over, adding a little more butter to the pan if needed.

3. Cook the sandwiches until the cheese is melted, about 5 minutes more. Repeat with the remaining ingredients for a total of 4 sandwiches.

Note: Sometimes I like to add cooked bacon in the sandwich. Place on top of the cheese topped bread and then top with the other slice of bread.

# lively lemony lemonade

7 LEMONS

1½ CUPS (340 G)
  GRANULATED SUGAR

1½ CUPS (375 ML) WATER

2 CUPS (500 ML) COLD WATER

1 CUP SLICED STRAWBERRIES,
  AS GARNISH

1 LEMON, WASHED AND
  THINLY SLICED, AS GARNISH

1. Wash the lemons well and finely grate 1 or 2 of them to obtain 1 tablespoon lemon zest. In a nonreactive saucepan, combine the lemon zest, sugar, and 1½ cups (375 ml) water. Bring to a boil and stir constantly, while boiling, for 4 minutes. Remove from the heat and let cool completely.

2. Juice the 7 lemons and pour the juice over a sieve into a pitcher. Add the cooled lemon syrup, cover, and refrigerate until cold.

3. To serve, add the 2 cups (500 ml) cold water to the lemon mixture and stir well. Pour the lemonade over ice into glasses and garnish with the strawberries and lemon slices, if desired.

## FUN FACT!

Be there as scientists discover the answers to some of today's most important questions in atmosphere, climate, and ocean research. *Explorer of the Seas* is equipped with state-of-the-art technology used by scientists from the University of Miami's Rosenstiel School of Marine and Atmospheric Science. Both children and adults alike can tour the laboratory and have access to two interactive exploration centers.

# turtle explorers
## caramel-fudge brownies

YIELD: 16 SQUARES

5 OUNCES (142 G)
UNSWEETENED CHOCOLATE,
CHOPPED (1 CUP)

1/2 CUP (115 G) UNSALTED
BUTTER

1/2 CUP (115 G) VEGETABLE
SHORTENING

3 EXTRA-LARGE EGGS

3 CUPS (675 G) GRANULATED
SUGAR

1 CUP (110 G) ALL-PURPOSE
FLOUR

13 OUNCES (368 G) CARAMELS,
UNWRAPPED (ABOUT 45)

1/3 CUP (75 ML) EVAPORATED
MILK

12 OUNCES (340 G) SEMISWEET
CHOCOLATE CHIPS

1/3 CUP CHOPPED WALNUTS
OR PECANS

1. Preheat the oven to 350°F (180°C). Lightly coat a 9 x 13-inch (22.5 x 32.5-cm) baking pan with butter.

2. Place the chocolate, butter, and shortening in the top of a double boiler set over 1 inch (2.5 cm) of simmering (not boiling) water. Whisk until the chocolate is smooth and no small lumps remain. Remove the mixture from the hot water (keep the water simmering). Let cool.

3. In a mixing bowl, combine the eggs and sugar. With an electric mixer, beat until pale in color, about 5 to 10 minutes, stopping 2 or 3 times to scrape down the sides of the bowl. With a rubber spatula, fold in the chocolate mixture. Sift the flour over the batter and fold it in just until incorporated (do not overmix).

4. Pour 3/4 of the batter into the prepared baking dish and bake for 6 minutes. Meanwhile, melt the caramels with the evaporated milk in the top of the double boiler set over the simmering water.

5. After 6 minutes, remove the brownies from the oven and sprinkle with the chocolate chips and nuts. Pour the melted caramel over the top and spoon the remaining brownie batter over the surface.

6. Bake the brownies for 30 minutes more. Let cool in the pan on a wire rack.

# dreamy devil's food cupcakes
## with buttercream frosting

YIELD: 18 CUPCAKES

### Cupcakes

BUTTER FOR GREASING

FLOUR FOR DUSTING

3 OUNCES (85 G) SEMISWEET
CHOCOLATE, CHOPPED

2$^1$/$_2$ CUPS (240 G) CAKE FLOUR

1$^3$/$_4$ CUPS (400 G) GRANULATED
SUGAR

1$^3$/$_4$ TEASPOONS BAKING SODA

1 TEASPOON SALT

$^2$/$_3$ CUP (150 G) UNSALTED
BUTTER, SOFTENED

1$^1$/$_3$ CUPS (325 ML)
BUTTERMILK, AT ROOM
TEMPERATURE

1 TEASPOON PURE VANILLA
EXTRACT

2 LARGE EGGS, AT ROOM
TEMPERATURE

1. Preheat the oven to 350°F/180°C. Coat 18 muffin cups with butter and dust with flour, or line with paper cupcake liners. Set aside.

2. Place the chocolate in the top of a double boiler set over 1 inch (1.5 cm) of simmering (not boiling) water. Whisk until smooth and no small lumps remain. Turn off the heat and remove the mixture from the hot water. Let cool to room temperature.

3. In a medium mixing bowl, whisk the flour, sugar, baking soda, and salt. In a large mixing bowl, beat the butter until fluffy. Add the flour mixture, 1 cup (250 ml) of the buttermilk, and vanilla. With an electric mixer, beat at high speed for 2 minutes, stopping 2 or 3 times to scrape down the sides of the bowl.

4. Add the eggs, melted chocolate, and remaining $^1$/$_3$ cup (75 ml) buttermilk. Beat for 1 minute more. Pour the batter into the muffin cups filling them two-thirds full and bake for 20 to 25 minutes, or until a skewer inserted in the center comes out clean. Let cool.

### Frosting

$^1$/$_2$ CUP (115 G) UNSALTED BUTTER, SOFTENED

2 TEASPOONS PURE VANILLA EXTRACT

3 TABLESPOONS HEAVY OR LIGHT CREAM

1 POUND (450 G) CONFECTIONERS' SUGAR

1 LARGE BAG M&Ms OR 1 JAR CHOCOLATE SPRINKLES

1. In a large bowl, combine the butter, vanilla, cream, and sugar. With an electric mixer, beat at high speed until fluffy, adding more cream if necessary.

2. Spread the tops of the cooled cupcakes with the frosting. Before the frosting dries and sets, decorate each cupcake with M&Ms or chocolate sprinkles.

# strawberry celebration

## Cake

BUTTER FOR GREASING

6 LARGE EGGS

3/4 CUP (170 G) PLUS 1 TABLESPOON
  GRANULATED SUGAR

1 1/2 TEASPOONS PURE VANILLA EXTRACT

1 1/4 CUPS (140 G) ALL-PURPOSE FLOUR,
  PLUS EXTRA FOR DUSTING

1 TEASPOON BAKING POWDER

1/2 TEASPOON SALT

1. Preheat the oven to 350°F (180°C). Coat two 9-inch (22.5 cm) cake pans with butter. Dust the pans with a little flour; tilt to coat and tap out the excess.

2. Combine the eggs and sugar in a medium bowl. With an electric mixer, beat at medium speed until very thick and light, about 2 minutes, stopping 2 or 3 times to scrape down the sides of the bowl. Add the vanilla and mix until incorporated.

3. Sift the flour, baking powder, and salt into the egg mixture and gently fold them in until just mixed. Divide the batter evenly between the 2 pans and bake for 30 minutes, or until the cakes spring back when lightly touched. Transfer the pans to a wire rack and let cool for 10 minutes. Run a knife around the edge of each pan and turn the cakes out onto the rack to cool completely.

## Strawberry Filling

2 PINTS STRAWBERRIES, RINSED AND WELL DRAINED

1/3 CUP (75 G) GRANULATED SUGAR

Hull and chop enough strawberries to equal 1 cup chopped; set the remainder aside. In a small saucepan, combine the chopped strawberries and the sugar. Mash the berries with the sugar a bit and then place over low heat. Cook, stirring constantly, for 3 minutes. Remove from the heat and let cool completely. (Can be made up to 1 day ahead; cover and chill until ready to use.)

## To Assemble

1 1/2 CUPS (375 ML) HEAVY WHIPPING CREAM

4 TO 6 TABLESPOONS GRANULATED SUGAR

1. With a serrated knife, cut each cake in half to make 2 layers each. With an electric mixer, whip the cream, gradually adding the sugar until the cream holds soft peaks and the sugar is incorporated.

2. Transfer 2 cups whipped cream to a bowl and fold in the cooked chopped strawberries. Reserve the remaining plain whipped cream. Place a cake layer bottom side down on a cake plate and spread with one-third of the strawberry cream filling. Continue to stack layers with filling in between, ending with a cake layer's flat "bottom side" up.

3. Spread the top layer of the cake with the reserved plain whipped cream, spreading any remaining cream on the sides if desired. Slice or quarter the reserved strawberries and arrange them decoratively on top of the cake. Refrigerate for 30 minutes before serving.

# photography credits

Herb Schmitz, International Photography, London

Richard Klapka of Avanti, a St. Ives Group (pages 2, 26, 31, 42, 145)

Foodpix/©Steve Cohen (page 72)

Envision/©Agence Top (page 114)

Foodpix/©Alison Miksch (page 126)

Foodpix/©Bill Boch (page 148)

Morton Tadder, product shots (pages 14, 46, 74, 99, 143, 168)


Page 176: Subjects photographed from left to right are Jamie Reid, Julie and David Goldstein, Kristina Sodamin, Bianca Farquharson, and Ariana Gomez.


FOODSTYLING

Pat Doyle, International Photography and Design, London and Rudi Sodamin, Food Sensation Enterprises, Coral Gables, Florida

Kim Hernandez, Floral Gallery, Miami, Florida and Dee Gretzler, Royal Caribbean International, Miami, Florida (pages 2, 26, 31, 42, 145)

# index